Elbridge Streeter Brooks

The American soldier

Being the story of the fighting-man of America

Elbridge Streeter Brooks

The American soldier
Being the story of the fighting-man of America

ISBN/EAN: 9783337147532

Printed in Europe, USA, Canada, Australia, Japan

Cover: Foto ©ninafisch / pixelio.de

More available books at **www.hansebooks.com**

ON THE RAMPARTS.

"Hurrah! hurrah! it is our home where'er thy colors fly,
We win with thee the victory, or in thy shadow die!"

AMERICAN SOLDIER

BEING THE STORY OF THE FIGHTING-MAN
OF AMERICA, FROM CONQUISTADOR TO
ROUGH RIDER; FROM 1492 TO 1900 • • •

BY

ELBRIDGE S. BROOKS

AUTHOR OF "THE AMERICAN SAILOR," "THE AMERICAN INDIAN," "THE TRUE
STORY OF THE UNITED STATES," "THE CENTURY BOOK
FOR YOUNG AMERICANS," ETC., ETC.

NEW AND REVISED EDITION

BOSTON
LOTHROP PUBLISHING COMPANY

PREFACE.

The simple story of the American soldier has never yet been told. Whoever wishes to know him as a man must study numerous confusing episodes, search through voluminous histories or sift out the man from the material in the crowding records of innumerable battles.

This is more labor than the busy American cares to undertake, much as he may delight in the records of American valor and American endeavor. It is to attempt this for him, to draw from the mass of material already in print the character and achievements of the fighting man of America even from the earliest times and to present them in consecutive and connected narrative that this book has been undertaken.

The description of battles and the causes of wars have not been entered into. These may be found and studied in detail in any one of the many excellent histories of the United States with which the libraries and homes of America abound. In this book the American soldier as an individual is depicted for the enlightenment and inspiration of Americans — young and old.

War is a terrible necessity. Looked at from the standpoint of humanity there is about it neither picturesqueness, nobility, romance nor delight; it is but the emphasis of man's inhumanity to man. And yet there is another point of view. War has been in the history of the world alike civilizer, peacemaker and uplifter. There could have been no progress for the race had the element of strife been lacking. The efforts of those heroic souls

"Who have dared for a high cause to suffer, resist, fight — if need be to die,"

have rung the death-knell of tyranny and moved the world forward toward a broader freedom.

And so, through all the years that have witnessed the evolution of the American Republic, the American soldier has been a prime factor in this development. His valor has illumined history, his steadfastness has redeemed failure, his loyalty has glorified success. It is for us as Americans to remember our debt to the heroes of Louisburg and Quebec, of Lexington and Saratoga and Yorktown, of Lundy's Lane and New Orleans, of Shiloh and Gettysburg and Appomattox, of El Caney and San Juan and Manila. Without their efforts there would have been no nation of freemen with sons ready to defend its honor and its life, no America to stand well at the fore to make its name the symbol of progress, protection, and glory.

CONTENTS.

CHAPTER I.
AN OVERTURE OF STRIFE 11

CHAPTER II.
THE CONQUISTADORES 32

CHAPTER III.
COLONIAL FIGHTING-MEN 56

CHAPTER IV.
MINUTE-MEN AND CONTINENTALS 78

CHAPTER V.
SOLDIERS OF LIBERTY 98

CHAPTER VI.
THE TROOPS OF DISCONTENT 121

CHAPTER VII.
A LEADERLESS WAR 143

CHAPTER VIII.
WARS AND RUMORS OF WAR 166

CHAPTER IX.
OVER THE MEXICAN BORDER 190

CHAPTER X.
HORSE, FOOT AND DRAGOON 214

CHAPTER XI.
BOYS OF 'SIXTY-ONE 232

CHAPTER XII.
FROM SHILOH TO APPOMATTOX 255

CHAPTER XIII.
BOOTS AND SADDLE 275

CHAPTER XIV.
THE BOYS OF '98 289

LIST OF ILLUSTRATIONS.

On the ramparts	L. J. Bridgman.	Frontis.
		PAGE
Initial — A war chief of the Mound-Builders		11
Indians attacking the mounds		14
" He halted and turned toward the enemy "	L. J. Bridgman	21
" Death to the Mun-dua ! "		27
Initial — A Conquistador		32
De Soto		34
" For Santiago and Spain ! "		37
Coronado's march	L. J. Bridgman	43
The first white man		53
The revolt of the train-bands	W. T. Smedley	60
Franklin as a private	L. J. Bridgman	65
A muster of Colonial militia on Boston Common	F. T. Merrill	73
" They hung on the skirts of the retreat "	Hy. Sandham	82
Green Mountain Boys on the march	L. J. Bridgman	85
The minute-men	Hy. Sandham	87
" The British are coming ! "	L. J. Bridgman	93
The Cambridge elm		96
The battle of Oriskany		103
Marion and his men	L. J. Bridgman	105
Washington reviewing the Continental Army		112
(From a painting by J. S. Thompson.)		
A garrison of two	L. J. Bridgman	117
" Peace by no means brought satisfaction "		123
" No fees, no executions, no sheriff ! "		129
Sentinel and ploughman		133
The battle of Tippecanoe	L. J. Bridgman	135
Anthony Wayne		139
Initial — James Wilkeson		143
At work on the fortifications in 1812		147
Captain Hindman at Fort George	L. J. Bridgman	153
Packenham's charge		158

LIST OF ILLUSTRATIONS.

Andrew Jackson		163
The backwoods soldiers		169
In the "anti-rent war"		182
Caricaturing the militia	*L. J. Bridgman*	185
The battle of Buena Vista	*L. J. Bridgman*	201
Marcy's perilous march	*L. J. Bridgman*	223
Good-by		225
Our brother the enemy	*L. J. Bridgman*	241
In the recruiting office		246
Working for the soldiers		251
Initial — The heat of battle	*Kemble*	255
Stannard's charge at Gettysburg		258
"Do you want to live forever?"		263
Morgan's raiders		267
After the battle	*Kemble*	271
"The home-coming of the Southern soldiers"	*Kemble*	278
Custer's last stand	*L. J. Bridgman*	283
At Guasimas		299

THE AMERICAN SOLDIER.

THE AMERICAN SOLDIER.

CHAPTER I.

AN OVERTURE OF STRIFE.

WITHIN that section of Southern Ohio where now stretches the pleasant County of Ross, there was enacted, a thousand years ago, a strange and stirring scene.

Against the almost inky blackness of an autumn night blazed up suddenly, with flash and flare, the climbing flame of a beacon fire. Its fitful glare, swayed, now this way and now that, by the keen November blasts, threw into sudden relief a looming watch-tower and a long line of frowning battlements that, topped with a ragged palisade, crested a sharply rising hill and stretched far away into the encircling gloom.

Another and yet another flaming beacon answer the summons of fire. One to the right and one to the left, and each a mile or more away from the central beacon, they light up the inky night. There comes a stir behind those walls of stone. The sharp, quick rallying cry sounds out. A long line of hurrying forms spring to the solid ramparts, which, rising to the height of ten feet, and with a width of more than thirty feet, afford standing place and fighting room for an army of defenders.

Behind the palisades they gather, wary and watchful, with bows drawn and spears poised for the fling. Schooled to the ways of savage warfare the night surprise has found them ready and alert. They live upon their arms.

From the watchers on the outer towers comes now the shrill cry of warning. They see the foe. Beyond the flickering rim of light a mass of crowding forms has been descried — a host of naked, be-feathered warriors, dodging here and there behind the giant tree-trunks, or drawing stealthily nearer to the rising wall of that towering hill-fort.

And now with a long, rising whoop of defiance that grows to a terrible and blood-curdling yell as, one after another, the myriad throats of that beleaguering host take up the cry, the mass of naked warriors rush madly within the glare of the beacon fire and discharge a storm of arrows against the palisades. From the watchful defenders comes an answering shower of arrows and of spears, while through the central entrance swarm out in sudden sortie an attacking force of stalwart fighting men.

These defenders of the beleaguered fort are dressed, each, in a belted blouse of woven cloth that falls nearly to the knee. The left arm of each long-haired soldier upholds a matted shield; his right hand firmly grasps a long and deadly spear. Their bravest war-chief leads the sortie out. A leathern buckler, edged with silver and gleaming with its copper boss, protects his breast; an iron sword, broad and sharply-pointed, waves above his head in encouragement and command, and at his side dangles its copper scabbard.

In close array and with something of martial order the soldiers of the fort dash on to the charge, following the feathered plume and brandished sword of their gallant chief. Straight into that host of beleaguering savages they dash, regardless of the flying arrow and the whirling hatchet. Then, with yell and whoop, true to the tactics of savage strife, the horde of naked assailants disappears in the gloom only to swarm again before some less defended point — there to let fly their cloud of arrows at the defenders behind the palisades.

Through the long night again and again are the assault and the defense, the sortie, flight and fresh attack renewed. Then, with the dawn, the beleaguering host fades away into the forest fastnesses. And, as the morning sun rises above that Ohio hill, the wearied warriors within the fortified town prostrate themselves toward the east and offer their thanks and sacrifices to the great sun-god who has given them the victory.

Thus, then, as the curtain of the centuries is rolled aside for us, do we obtain a glimpse of the earliest American soldier — the earliest, at least, worthy the name of soldier, who with something of order and the show and circumstance of war could do such desperate battle in defense of fortress and of home. It is, for us, an insight into the ways and manners of that long-vanished and mysterious people known now but vaguely under the uncertain name of the Mound Builders — a name given only because of the fast disappearing ruins of the marvelous works of engineering skill that they so long and valiantly defended against the ceaseless assaults of a relentless savagery.

The fighting-man is as old as the human race. The combative quality in men and nations has never lacked a representative. Wherever rivalry has been engendered or ambition has had birth the man of war has ever and always resulted. "All antiquity," says Renan, "was cruel." No nation exists that does not rest on the foundation stones of strife and blood.

The American people form no exception to the rule. Their

INDIANS ATTACKING THE MOUNDS.

prehistoric story is written in strife and told in eras of conflict. Evolved from savagery through long centuries of struggle and of warfare the early Americans were ever at strife and grew, apparently, only through the law of the survival of the fittest.

The strong man and the war chief were leaders and rulers in our prehistoric days.

Invaded mound and rifled tumulus yield, always, among their meager spoil the inevitable arrow-head of flint or chalcedony or hard obsidian. The shell-heaps and "kitchen-middens," that speak of a stage of human existence yet nearer to the brute, disclose, amid their crumbling dust, hatchet and arrow-head, dagger and knife of rough-hewed stone, while, alongside the half-fossilized human remains that speak of an almost fabulous antiquity for the American race, have been found the stone war-club and the beveled lance-head that tell, ever, the self-same story of conflict and of blood.

Dating thus backward to the very beginning of things the American fighting-man has always been a product of American soil. There can, however, but little real identity attach to his story, until, from the uncertain testimony of the Western mounds and from the more credible legends of the red Indian who was the heir of all the ages that here preceded him we obtain our first tangible impression of the early American "soldier."

And a soldier this same red barbarian was, despite his forest tactics and his ignorance of the real "art" of war.

War was the Indian's second nature; it was his business, his pastime and his life. To attain the eagle's feather was his highest aim; to achieve the seat of the war chief by the suffrages of his comrades was the end of all ambition. The brave at home was but a lazy fellow, scorning manual labor and deeming toil as unsuited to one whose duty it was to become a hero.

But on the war-path and in the forest foray he was a far different creature. Then, no toil was too severe, no exertion was too harsh. Intent on the surprise and capture of his hereditary foeman he brought into play all his knowledge of woodcraft, all his varied schooling in skill and cunning. With untiring patience and with an ability that was almost genius he read the language of broken twig and trodden grass, of disturbed stream and of uncertain trail. The story of the intertribal wars of the American Indian, could this but be fitly told, would possess as much of courage, of endurance and of artifice as is to be found in any mythical tradition of Troy's ensanguined plains or in the stirring legends of the Golden Fleece.

The Roman Horatius, swimming the turbid Tiber, is fully paralleled by that brave Ojibway father who, burning to revenge the death of his warrior son, flung himself — "with his harness on his back" — into the vaster waters of the "Great Lake" (Superior) and swam a distance of over two miles, from the island of La Pointe to the mainland, to join in the deadly battle that his tribe was waging against the hostile Dakotas.

Ga-geh-djo-wa the Seneca — the warrior with the heron's plume in his crest — is the fiery Henry of Navarre of the American forests. The braves of the warlike Iroquois outshone in valor and endurance the legionaries of a triumphant Cæsar, the spearmen of an Attila or an Alexander. "When you go to war," runs the old Ute proverb, "every one you meet is an enemy; kill all!" Was not this, too, the policy of a Hannibal, a Pompey and an Alaric?

Among the Indians in the old days there were no impressments, there were no conscripts. All were volunteers. The American warrior was a free man.

But the enlistment was unique. The plan of operations was according to a set form, as binding as were ever those of any marshal of France or any paladin of Spain. Let this glimpse at the military life of the Omahas show us the aboriginal

American soldier as he existed among the pre-Columbian tribes of the higher order of intelligence.

Wa-ba-ska-ha the Ponka had suffered a great wrong at the hands of the Pawnees. His honor and the honor of his tribe demanded swiftest vengeance. But the initial move could only come from Wa-ba-ska-ha himself. He and none other must organize a war party.

With his face bedaubed with clay, to indicate his grief, Wa-ba-ska-ha wandered among the lodges of his people. And as he wandered he cried, thus and often, to Wa-kan-da, the protecting spirit of the Omahas: "O, Wa-kan-da! though others have injured me, do thou help me!" And the people, hearing his appeal, said: "What! would you lead out a war-party, Wa-ba-ska-ha? Who has wronged you? Let us hear your story." And then he would recite his wrongs until all his tribe was acquainted with his story.

Thereupon four messengers, friends of Wa-ba-ska-ha, ran as criers through the village, calling out the name of each warrior and bidding him come to an assembly. And when all the chiefs and warriors were gathered together, the war-pipe was filled and Wa-ba-ska-ha, stretching out his hands in appeal to his people, said, "Pity me, my brothers; do for me as you think best."

Then said the chief who filled the sacred pipe: "If you are willing, O warriors, for us to take vengeance on the Pawnees, put this pipe to your lips. If you are not willing, put it not to your lips." And every man placed the sacred pipe to his lips and smoked it. Thus they volunteered for the foray, and Wa-ba-ska-ha was glad. Then said the chief, "Now make a final decision. Say you, O warriors, when shall we take this vengeance?" And one of the warriors made answer: "O

chief, the summer comes; let us eat our food. When the leaves
fall we will take vengeance on the Pawnees."

This was the voice of the whole assembly. But Wa-ba-ska-ha
would not let the matter rest. Through the whole summer, by
day and by night, and even while they accompanied the people
on the summer hunt, his four messengers, or captains, were
continually crying out: "O Wa-kan-da! pity me! Help me in
that which keeps me angry." And they would fast through all
the day; only in the night would they eat and drink.

Then, when the hunt was over, Wa-ba-ska-ha gave the war-
party a feast at his lodge; and the four captains sat before the
entrance while two messengers sat on either side the door.
And as they ate and drank and sang the sacred war-songs they
determined upon what day the war-path should be taken. And
the five sacred bags, filled with red, blue and yellow feathers,
and consecrated to the war-god, were distributed among the
chiefs or leaders of the clans of the tribe.

The day having been set the leaders of the war-party selected
their lieutenants and assigned to each of the chiefs of the tribe
a company of twenty warriors. Secretly and at night all the
warriors who had volunteered for the fight slipped out of their
lodges and each company met its chief at a rendezvous agreed
upon. Here they blackened their faces with charcoal or mud
and fasted for four days. And when the four days were past
they washed their faces, put plumes in their hair and gathering
around the principal captains watched the opening of the
sacred bags. Twenty policemen were appointed to keep the
stragglers to their duty and four scouts were sent ahead, keeping from two to four miles in advance of the party.

Directly after breakfast the war-party commenced its march.
First came two of the minor captains, bearing the sacred bags.

A hundred yards behind marched the chiefs of the tribe, and following them came the warriors. Frequent halts for rest were made but, when resting, the party must always keep close together to avoid surprise.

When the scouts had met the captains at a point agreed upon and made their report as to traces of the enemy or of game other scouts were appointed in their place and the march went on.

So, under bright skies or beneath cloudy ones, the Ponkas advanced toward their vengeance. Along the forest trails and across the grassy meadows, ablaze with the nodding flowers of the early fall, they pressed straight on. But neither sky nor flower won any thought from them. And as they neared their foe those who were hot for revenge grew still more fierce and counseled their comrades to valorous deeds. Chief among these was Wa-ba-ska-ha; for as the warriors marched he sprang in a furious dance before and around them, singing thus:

> "O make us quicken our steps!
> O make us quicken our steps!
> Ho, O war-chief! When I see him
> I shall have my heart's desire!
> O war-chief, make us quicken our steps!"

And after he had thus sung he shouted to the listening warriors: "Ho, brothers, I have said truly that I shall have my heart's desire! Truly, brothers, they shall not detect me at all. I am rushing on without any desire to spare a life. If I meet one of the foe I will not spare him."

Each night when they camped for rest and sleep the four scouts would go out about a mile from the camping ground — one toward the enemy's country, one to the rear, and one to either side of the camp. And, before the warriors lay down to sleep, the "*mikasi*" or coyote dance, to keep up the spirits of all, would be engaged in by all except the captains.

Before sunrise, each morning, the camp was awake ; breakfast was hastily eaten and the day's march resumed. At last the wary scouts far in advance sighted the village of the enemy and hastening back made their report. The sacred bags were opened, the scalp yell was raised and each warrior boasted anew of how he should conduct himself when he met the foe. And here, as the height of courage, Na-jin-ti-ce, the chief, the friend of Wa-ba-ska-ha, changed his name before the battle and bade the crier so proclaim it. And the crier, lifting his hands first toward the skies and then dropping them toward the earth, thus proclaimed it : " Thou deity on either side, hear it ; hear ye that he has taken another name. He will take the name Nu-da-nax-a (Cries-for-the-war-path), halloo ! Ye big head-lands, I tell you and send my voice that ye may hear it, halloo ! Ye clumps of buffalo grass, I tell you and send it to you that ye may hear it, halloo ! Ye big trees, I tell you and send it to you that ye may hear it, halloo ! Ye birds of all kinds that walk and move on the ground, I tell you and send it to you that ye may hear it, halloo ! Ye small animals of different sizes, that walk and move on the ground, I tell you and send it to you that ye may hear it, halloo ! Thus have I sent to you to tell you, O ye animals ! Right in the ranks of the foe will he kill a very swift man and come back after holding him, halloo ! He has thrown away the name Na-jin-ti-ce and will take the name Nu-da-nax-a, halloo ! "

Now that the enemy had been discovered all was interest and action. The scouts were sent forward to count the lodges and discover whether the foemen were asleep or awake — for it was nightfall. Then one of the chiefs went himself to make a final

"HE HALTED AND TURNED TOWARD THE ENEMY."

examination. And at midnight, when all were ready, they moved stealthily forward; going by twenties, each warrior holding the hand of the man next him, they crawled toward the Pawnee village. Within arrow-shot of the village they halted, talking in whispers and exhorting each other to deeds of bravery. Just at daybreak, the leading war-chief drew his bow and sent an arrow toward the sleeping foe. Its flight could be distinctly seen by all the watching warriors. The time for the attack had arrived. The war-chief waved the sacred bag four times toward the enemy, he shouted his war-cry and at once the warriors, raising the scalp-yell, let fly their arrows.

That terrible yell, familiar to Indian ears, roused the sleepers. Snatching at their ever-ready weapons they rushed out into the chill morning air. Too late! The surprise was complete. Every surrounding tree-trunk sheltered a Ponka brave. Now from this quarter, now from that dashed out a hostile foeman to strike down or capture an unwary Pawnee. First to strike down and first to drag away his fallen foeman was Wa-ba-ska-ha. His vengeance had begun.

For an instant the Pawnees gained the advantage. Massing themselves for a rush they dashed against their enemy discharging their arrows as they ran.

The Indian could seldom stand before a combined assault. His tactics were those of ambuscade and covert. The Ponkas fled before the Pawnee onset. But even as they ran Wa-ba-ska-ha heard the cry: " Nu-da-nax-a is killed!"

The bond of kinship was stronger than the fear of capture. He halted and turned toward the enemy. "Ho! I will stop running," he said. He dashed headlong into the very thick of the foe and, across the dead body of his friend and kinsman, Wa-ba-ska-ha fell fighting. His vengeance was completed.

But one such brave turn as his stayed the tide of retreat. The Pawnees fled at his approach and the Ponkas, following after, scattered or captured their routed foemen.

The death of the two friends ended the conflict. The Omahas, to which race the Ponkas belonged, never continued a fight after a chief had been killed. Gathering up their spoil and their captives the Ponka warriors turned homeward and the foray was over. Within the shadow of their own lodges the victory was celebrated with song and dance, the rewards for bravery were distributed among the warriors who had most highly distinguished themselves and the deeds and deaths of Nu-da-nax-a and Wa-ba-ska-ha were loudly sung. They had gone in glory to the rewards of Wa-kan-da.

Such heroic deaths as were those of these two friends were not uncommon among the barbaric warriors of the American forests. The story of Damon and Pythias could find frequent parallels in Indian tradition. The "companion warriors" of the prairie tribes, the "fellowhood" of the Wyandots, the curious rites of the Zuni "Priesthood of the Bow"—these and similar phases of Indian military life, of which the study of American ethnology affords us frequent glimpses, are proof of a methodical system of war training and a standard of martial heroism among the naked warriors of the Western world that not even the days of Roman prowess or the later era of a brutal knight-errantry could surpass. The cultured Natchez of the Mississippi Delta had regularly established schools for the military training of their youth; Toltec and Aztec, alike, laid especial stress upon the war-training of their boys; and in the farther north Omaha and Iroquois, bravest of the forest races, gave the military education of their youth into the charge of efficient and established teachers.

Schooled thus to war and warlike ways the American Indian was a born soldier. A barbarian rather than a savage there was a method in his every move on war-path and in ambuscade and battle. And this was based on a peculiar school of tactics that was by no means the brutal hack and hew of the savage fighter. His art of war was built upon cunning and hedged about with strategy. It called for a course of fast and vigil that suggests the preliminaries of battle undertaken by the barbarian fighters of the so-called days of chivalry. The "knight of Arthur's court" and the brave of the Mohawk Valley differed but little in their ways of war. True, the Indian warrior did not ride out to the slaughter of undefended inferiors sheathed in steel and guarded at every point by the ingenuity of the blacksmith and the work of the ironmonger. His was the more heroic equality of man to man, unhelmeted, naked and free. His regimentals were his hideous daubs of mud or clay, his weapons the stone hatchet, the knotty war-club and the sharpened arrow, his oriflamme the heron's crest or the eagle's feather, his torture-chamber the forest clearing and the sacrificial fire.

At once the exigencies and the rivalries of his life made war an ever-present necessity; but it was also an ever-present opportunity. His heroism was lofty, but it implied craft and cunning. The warrior who could circumvent was a greater brave than he who simply shot to kill. Glooskap the Algonquin divinity was at once fighter and conjurer. Atotarho the Iroquois war-god was wizard and warrior as well; while even the mythical Hiawatha was quite as much the wonderful magician as he was champion and diplomat.

Centuries ago there lived on the rocky shores of Lake Superior a numerous and warlike people known as the Mun-dua. Presumably of Dakota stock this Indian tribe was fierce and cunning, relentless and strong. Into their homeland, forced westward by the all-conquering Iroquois, came the Ojibways, a people of Algonquin blood. For years the newcomers lived in continual terror of their ferocious neighbors. To hunt in the shadows of the Northern forests, to fish on the waters of the Great Fresh Sea meant for the Ojibways constant anxiety, and the risk of capture and the stake.

To a people who had faced the Iroquois in fight such a state of vassalage was not to be endured. In union there is strength, reasoned the badgered Ojibways. Other tribes, their neighbors as well, lived like them in terror of the Mun-dua. To these the Ojibways suggested a confederacy of annihilation. The chiefs in council pledged their warriors to the attempt, and the wampum and the war-club were sent in summons among the lodges of the confederated tribes.

Volunteers responded from every village. The preliminary rites of fast and vigil, of mystic medicine and sacred dance were all performed, and on the appointed day there streamed from out the rendezvous the long and wavering line of a great war-party. Preceded by their watchful scouts and led on by their tribal chiefs, the confederated warriors stealthily threaded the narrow trails of the mighty forest, drawing nearer and yet nearer to the town of their common enemy, determined, so the record tells us, "to put out their fire forever."

The "great town" of the Mun-dua, protected by palisades, topped a sightly hill that overlooked the mighty lake. From their outlooks the Mun-dua spied out the advance of the besiegers; but confident of their own prowess they laughed the laugh of scorn and made no movement to check their rebellious vassals.

AN OVERTURE OF STRIFE.

The encircling forest poured out its host of besiegers. On every side of the Mun-dua town, save where the waters of the Great Fresh Sea broke on the rocky beach, the Ojibways and their allies swarmed before the palisades. With every mark and gesture of Indian defiance they shouted their challenge to the foe. They danced and sang, they raised the scalp-halloo and shot their flights of arrows at the unyielding wall. And yet the Mun-dua gave no reply; they sent out no force of warriors to answer the defiance of their vassals.

At last, after the first fury of the besiegers had expended itself in war-whoop and harmless arrow-flight, the gates of the village opened and forth came, to scatter the presumptuous rebels, not the warriors of the tribe, but the boys of the Mun-dua. The Indian contempt for an inferior foeman could no farther go. But the indignant allies, turning their

"DEATH TO THE MUN-DUA!"

bows into rods, beat back the boys of the Mun-dua into the lodges of their mothers.

"So; these slaves need harsher chastisement," said the chieftains of the Mun-dua. "They shall have it!" And on the next day they set out against their besiegers the young men of the tribe, warriors in training only, and bade them prove their fitness for the war-path on the bodies of these audacious rebels. But they knew not the valor of the Ojibways. Stung to a mighty rage by the insolence of their would-be masters these old Iroquois fighters rushed against the youngsters sent upon them and driving them back through the open gates pursued them to the very lintels of their lodges. Thus, forcing the palisades, they held in conquest half the invaded town.

Then, at last, the chiefs of the Mun-dua awoke to their danger. These were not cowards and cravens that had dared to rise against their power, but men; and like men they must be met. The warriors sprang to arms: scarred veterans of the war-path, valorous braves of the foray, stalwart chieftains of the war parties and the council-fires — they rallied now to repel an invader they could no longer affect to despise. They smeared themselves with the war-paint, they sang the inspiriting scalp-song, they anxiously consulted the sacred medicine-bags, and, strong of purpose, they flung themselves upon their foe.

That day the fight was to the death. All the deepest passions, all the dearest hopes of man — be he civilized or savage — were met in deadliest strife. To the Ojibways and their allies the struggle was for release from servitude, for vengeance and for glory; to the Mun-dua, brought at last to bay, it was for mastery, for home, even for life itself.

All the desperate arts, all the daring risks, all the deadliest devices of Indian warfare met or were attempted upon the slopes of that blood-stained hill above the inland sea. The fight was hand to hand; and the traditions say that never in all the story of Indian warfare was ever fight that exceeded the fierceness of that battle by the Great Fresh Sea.

But victory rested with the Ojibways. Step by step they drove the warlike Mun-dua back — back from the palisades, back over the hill-top, back to the very edge of the bluff on which the village stood. The women and children, dreading capture, threw themselves into the lake, the ground was strewn with the bodies of the bravest chiefs and warriors of the Mun-dua; of all that powerful tribe scarcely a handful was left. Silently and sadly, but swiftly as their desperate circumstances demanded, the defeated remnant, under cover of a dense lake fog that arose as if to shield them, turned and fled from their relentless enemies and their field of defeat.

But the fog was even more treacherous than their human foe. For when, after a day and night of weary flight, the fog at last left them, behold! there they stood on the very hill-slope that had held their conquered town and within full view of their now jubilant foemen. "It is the will of the Great Spirit that we should perish," said the aged chief who alone of all their valiant men of war, remained to lead them; "let us die like men." Once more they turned at bay. But they were spent and worn while their enemies were refreshed and strong. Resistance was useless. Chief and warrior fell side by side, and when the dispirited remnant turned once more to flight they were surrounded and captured. Incorporated, as was the Indian custom, within the victorious tribe the captives became Ojibways and the name of the Mun-dua disappeared forever from the page of Indian story.

The legends and traditions of those barbaric confederacies that but sparsely dotted the vast North American continent four centuries ago are marked throughout by just such paragraphs as this. Brutal and relentless, shrewd and crafty, actuated by all the selfishness and by all the cunning that dominates the barbaric mind, the American Indian, judged from his own standards, was still a trained, a valiant and a veteran soldier. Had but the records of his years of supremacy in this old New World remained to us, as have the records of Goth and Vandal, Hun and Celt, we might be able to place in the galleries of heroism the portraits of American warriors as bold as Alaric, as relentless as Attila, as manly as Vercingetorix, as liberty-loving as Civilis, as stubborn in fight as those noble old Britons Cassivelaunus and Boadicea and Hereward the Wake.

Their weapons of warfare were as crude as were their military tactics. But both served the purpose of their time and gave victory to the bravest until matched against the more intelligent methods of the unconquerable white man. To as intelligent a use of these latter, the red warrior proved himself unequal. Schooled for centuries on a lower plane of effort and action the American Indian was entirely unable to assimilate the ways and the weapons of the mailed warriors from across the western sea. The military empire of Montezuma in the South, the forest despotism of the Iroquois in the North went down in defeat before the unattainable precision of Spanish arquebuse and English musket. So fell the Natchez, so fell Creek and Algonquin, Illinois and Ojibway. Conquered in war as in other matters by the intelligence that was already regenerating Europe the free warriors of the American forests yielded to the inevitable. The barbaric nobility of pre-Columbian days, unable to cope with the refined cruelties of the more powerful white man, speedily degenerated. Daring became brutality, and valor lapsed into mere ferocity; harassed and hunted, their cunning turned to treachery, their skill gave place to vindictiveness. Forced from lords of the land to vassals, serfs and hunted fugitives their war-record became now only a series of losing struggles against manifest destiny. The history of Indian warfare after the coming of the white man is but a sickening record of Christian duplicity and Indian atrocity.

Thus the old day of the earliest American soldier ends. The overture of strife that sounded through centuries of blood closes in the war-song of defeat. A new race of fighters from over the sea, mailed and gauntleted in shining steel now comes to take up the story of war, of conquest and of blood. The naked fighter of forest, plain and water-side gives place to the bearers of the crossletted banner and the next chapter in the story of the American soldier must be that of the cruel but valorous *Conquistador*.

CHAPTER II.

THE CONQUISTADORES.

THE foundations upon which American sovereignty was reared were laid in conflict and cemented with blood. In no other newly-discovered continent was the work of conquest so thorough, so comprehensive and so complete. Asia, though echoing for centuries to the tramp of conquering armies, is yet only fringed with the marks of Christian occupation. Africa, the seat of the earliest civilizations, has been for ages the "Dark Continent," the mystery of which Christian science and Christian conquest have hardly yet unlocked.

In America how different is the record. At once the genius, the cupidity and the daring of the brightest and bravest of Europe's adventurers saw in the new world unlimited fortunes to be won, deathless glory to be achieved and an unbounded empire to be had only for the taking.

And they came prepared to take. In every vessel, large or small, that followed the track marked out by Columbus and the

Cabots across the stormy western ocean came Spanish hidalgo, French chevalier and English noble armed for battle and for conquest.

It is true that the first of the white strangers who won renown on American shores were sailors rather than soldiers; navigators rather than conquerors. The sons of Eric the Northman and "their iron-armed and stalwart crew" were fighters, no doubt; Whittier says of them:

> "I see the gleam of axe and spear,
> The sound of smitten shields I hear,
> Keeping a harsh and fitting time
> To saga's chant and runic rhyme."

But they came to Markland and to Vinland more for discovery than for conquest; their brief and half-mythical occupation was one of peace and of uncertainty rather than of determination. Thorvald the Viking died under an Indian arrow near the present site of Boston. Karlsefne's fight with the "skraelings," as the Indians of Vinland were termed, was but a doubtful conflict. The historic valor of the vikings of saga and rune seems to have found no place in the legends of Vinland. The dragon-ships headed homeward and the Norse occupation of America was over almost before it had begun.

But in cabin and in forecastle on the fleets that followed the caravels of Columbus the admiral came men who were more soldier than sailor and more adventurer than either. The great admiral, himself, believed that he had discovered the gateway of the earthly paradise. His companions, contemporaries and successors — loyal sons of the Church and devout soldiers of the Cross — were confident that they had only to enter in to conquer and enjoy all the delights and all the boundless riches of the toil-free garden of Eden.

So over the sea they came. Castilian nobles brave in slashed silks and all the display of a powerful and punctilious court, grim old infidel-fighters in war-scarred coats of mail, gay young dons with the fluttering love-tokens of dark-eyed senoritas tucked jauntily into doublet or cap, impecunious hidalgos, down on their luck but confident of winning abundant fortune among the pagans whom the Lord had evidently created only to be the slaves and serfs of these high-toned gentlemen of Spain!

DE SOTO.

Amid the blare of trumpets and the roar of cannon they sailed away into the unknown. Confident, boastful and valorous their dreams were all of conquest; the possibility of defeat never entered into their calculations. So sailed the second expedition of Columbus, his seventeen vessels thronged with a brilliant following — "hidalgos of high rank, officers of the royal household and Andalusian cavaliers," schooled in arms and inspired with a passion for hardy achievements by the romantic wars of Granada; so sailed the armament of the valorous Ojeda, in ten ships fitted out by the purses of the confederated adventurers, bound for fame and fortune; so too in quest of empire went Pedro de Avila, called by men "the Fury of the Lord," and Diego de Nicuesa, the rival of the fiery Ojeda, who, "in gay and vaunting style," set out for the Golden Land whereon he needed only to set foot to win. So too sailed Ponce de Leon, "lord of Bimini and Adelantado of Florida," and Cortez, alcalde of Santiago, on the mission that was to make him famous; and last, but by no means the least, so sailed Hernando de Soto prepared for conquest and colonization.

How speedily all these gallant gentlemen and valorous hidalgos of Spain came to grief history only too graphically records. High hopes went down in wreck; fortune and empire proved but will-of-the-wisps; and only a fame strangely compounded of mighty valor and the most relentless brutality remains as their heritage. The world-seeking companions of Columbus one and all died the deaths of homeless wanderers; the gallant but reckless Ojeda, aspiring to an empire that should rival that of Alexander — than whom, says Charlevoix, " none had a heart more lofty, nor ambition more aspiring" — turned monk and died so poor that he had not even the small pittance needful to pay for his burial. Avila, cruel-minded to the last, rose to power in the New World but, deprived of his offices, lingered on, disgraced and forgotten, to the great age of ninety years. Nicuesa, after a career of romance and disaster almost unparalleled, was expelled from his governorship and seeking flight in a crazy brigantine was never heard of more. Ponce de Leon, soldier-like to the end, risked an empire that he was never to obtain and died from the avenging arrow of the warriors of that fair Land of Flowers he had hoped to enslave. Upon the tomb of this stout old cavalier stands the only record of one whom fate delighted to baffle : " Within this sepulcher rest the bones of a man who was a lion by name and still more by nature."

De Soto, bravest and most brutal of all, born for valor and swayed by greed, saw his gorgeous and gallant following die man by man beneath the arrows of an outraged people and the sharper wounds of hardship and disease. Wealth and fame, power and prestige alike deserted him and at last he died — a wandering outcast in the very wilderness that he had boasted would yield him the revenues of a richer Mexico and a more marvelous Peru.

The story of these gallant captains is but that of their comrades and successors. Hundreds and thousands, drawn from the very flower of Spanish chivalry, risked their all in a crusade that was to be, so they fondly imagined, more crowded with heroism and more gloriously golden in results than was that against the turbaned infidels of the Holy Land or the picturesque conflicts beneath the walls of Granada.

"The youth of the nation," says Mr. Irving, "bred up to daring adventure and heroic achievement, could not brook the tranquil and regular pursuits of common life, but panted for some new field of romantic enterprise . . . . . The Spanish cavalier embarked in the caravel of the discoverer. He carried among the trackless wildernesses of the New World the same contempt of danger and fortitude and suffering; the same restless, roaming spirit; the same passion for inroad and ravage, and vainglorious exploit; and the same fervent, and often bigoted zeal for the propagation of his faith, that had distinguished him during his warfare with the Moors. Instances in point will be found in the extravagant career of the daring Ojeda, particularly in his adventures along the coast of Terra Firma, and the wild shores of Cuba; in the sad story of the unfortunate Nicuesa, graced as it is with occasional touches of high-bred courtesy; in the singular cruise of that brave but credulous old cavalier, Juan Ponce de Leon, who fell upon the flowery coast of Florida in search after an imaginary fountain of youth; and above all, in the checkered fortunes of Vasco Nunez de Balboa, whose discovery of the Pacific Ocean forms one of the most beautiful and striking incidents in the history

"FOR SANTIAGO AND SPAIN'"

of the New World, and whose fate might furnish a theme of wonderful interest for a poem or a drama."

And what fighters they were. Not all their greed for gold, nor all their brutal ways, not all their vainglorious boastings, nor all the bigotry of their religious faith can force into the background their indomitable pluck, their valor or their fury in war. The golden banner of Spain may have flaunted in American breezes above superstition, fanaticism, avarice and cruelty, but beneath its folds fought also as valiant warriors, as courageous cavaliers, and as gallant gentlemen as ever drew sword for king, for glory and for renown.

As types of those commingled qualities that made up the picturesque *conquistador* of the sixteenth century three names stand clearly out from the dramatic story of those days of conflict and of blood: Alonso de Ojeda, the companion of Columbus, Pedro de Alvarado, the lieutenant of Cortez and Francisco Vasquez de Coronado the conqueror of New Mexico.

Ambitious, adventurous, daring, reckless and always oversanguine, Alonso de Ojeda was a born fighter. He early essayed the life of a soldier. Schooled to examples of valor as a page of the fiery duke of Medina Celi in the Moorish wars he was scarce more than a boy when he joined the second expedition of Columbus as gentleman-adventurer. From the first sight we have of him heading a band of ambitious young cavaliers across the mountains of San Domingo on a search for the warlike and powerful cacique whom men called "the Lord of the Golden House," to the very last glimpse that comes to us when, brought to bay in the streets of San Domingo, he fought single-handed the whole band of his would-be assassins, his story is one of continuous adventure and daring deeds. A perfect horseman and as gallant a cavalier as ever struck home for "Santiago and Spain!" he was as magnanimous as he was reckless; as open-handed in peace as he was irresistible in war.

His capture of Caonabo was a sample of his courage and recklessness. At the head of ten mailed and mounted followers he boldly dashed across the mountains and into the very presence of this fiery Carib chieftain — " the Lord of the Golden House." Though surrounded by dangers that suggested death at every turn, Ojeda prevailed upon Caonabo reluctantly to visit Columbus. Separating him from his extensive escort the Spaniard shrewdly induced the cacique to wear as bracelets a pair of glittering steel handcuffs. Binding his then unresisting prisoner upon the fleet horse he had been induced to mount, Ojeda and his followers galloped away from the swarm of astounded Caribs and bore the illustrious captive into the very camp of Columbus.

But recklessness is not leadership and the successful fighter can rarely prove a match for the scheming politician. Soldierly in bearing, dashing in devices, terrible in war, restless if not engaged in some daring and adventurous exploit, Ojeda was yet perpetually the dupe of some wily gold-getter, and was always as poor in purse as he was proud in spirit. Success never attended his endeavors by lining his pockets with the Carib gold that every Spaniard coveted. Wealth continually evaded him.

His indomitable spirit, his tireless vigor, his good comradeship, his ability as a captain, his great personal prowess and his unflagging striving for success were more than counterbalanced by his utter incompetency to rule where he had conquered, his bigotry, his useless hardihood, his scorn of caution, his wastefulness and his impatience of control. These latter all led to his downfall. "Good management and good fortune," says

Charlevoix, "forever failed him," and the very qualities that made Alonzo de Ojeda " one of the most fearless and aspiring of the band of Ocean chivalry that followed the footsteps of Columbus " combined, also, to make his life a failure and his career a tragedy.

Of a similar heroic strain but more wisely balanced was the famous Pedro de Alvarado. Stripped of all the bombastic romancing of the Spanish chroniclers, to whom this fiery young captain was almost a demi-god, Pedro de Alvarado still stands forth the very synonym of all that is most fascinating in the old-time fighter. As chivalrous as fearless, and as resistless as bold this friend and favorite lieutenant of Cortez added to a fiery nature a face and form that won for him admirers among both friends and foes. To the simple and superstitious Indians of Mexico this dashing cavalier, cased in armor and deftly guiding his galloping steed, seemed almost divine. To them he was To-na-ti-uh — the Child of the Sun — and in making him the hero of a most entertaining romance of the Conquest * General Wallace has but embodied in story many of the attributes that the conquered Aztecs ascribed to this paladin of the Mexican causeway, the brightest figure in the awful " night of sorrow."

Embarking as an adventurer almost before he had become a man this young soldier of fortune sailed over-sea from his home in Badajoz to the alluring Land of Promise. Speedily finding opportunity he was the first to bring to Cuba tidings of the wealth and power of the Mexico that was to make him famous. Following the banner of Cortez to the conquest of that half-mythical tropic empire Alvarado became, next to his

---

* " The Fair God ", or the Last of the 'Tzins." Lew Wallace. — A charming and altogether delightful story of the romantic conquest of Mexico.

general, the central figure of that historic conquest. A born leader of men he speedily rose to command and wherever opportunity for fighting occurred or hope of booty beckoned he was first on the field and established a reputation for daring and for valor wherever danger threatened or death appeared most imminent. His personal bravery and personal prowess, (displayed in such achievements as that famous leap across the bloody causeway that has now become historic) dwell longest with the lover of gallant deeds who reads his story and yields to the fascinations of his warlike feats, but the student of history sees beneath the knightly bearing the less attractive traits that were so often discoverable in the make-up of the *conquistador*.

For this brilliant fighter was far from god-like. He was greedy for gold, treacherous toward a trusting foeman, overbearing, arrogant and full of craft. "He had," says Prescott, who recounts with fervor all his great exploits, "a heart rash, rapacious and cruel." And when the Aztec nation fell and the Conquest was accomplished few contributed more toward making both fall and conquest bitter and unchristian than did this typical *conquistador*, this valiant "Child of the Sun," Pedro de Alvarado. It seems but a fitting retribution that his death in after years should have come in the hour of his defeat by these very Mexican Indians whom he had conquered and by an unsoldierly fall from his horse — one of those same strange and mysterious beasts upon whose back in earlier days this redoubtable To-na-ti-uh had been so irresistible.

Of a very different type and yet quite as distinctively a Spaniard was Francisco Vasquez de Coronado, the "conqueror" of New Mexico. No longer a young man this honest cavalier of Salamanca was of grave deportment, affable manners and of fair executive ability. Long residence in Mexico, where he was

CORONADO'S MARCH.

established in 1540 as governor of one of the western provinces, had given him acquaintance with the manners and disposition of the natives of that conquered land. The impetuosity of youth had given place to the caution and sedateness of middle age. A valiant and courageous gentleman, slow to decide and not always quick to act, he was watchful to prevent disaster, and while never courting danger, he was cool and brave in action when danger really came.

Such a leader was certain to command the respect of his followers, and Coronado seems to have had this and to have inspired also both the love and the confidence of his soldiers. Says one of them, Pedro de Casteneda the chronicler of his captain's wanderings: "Never was Spanish general in the Indies more beloved or better obeyed than he."

But grave, circumspect and valiant though he was Coronado seems to have been compounded of those strangely clashing elements that united in the Spanish fighter of those olden times. An unforgiving foeman, terrible in his revenges and contemptuous of the poor natives over whom he was either ruler or conqueror, Coronado was, above all, avaricious, superstitious and credulous to a degree, with an ever-ready ear for the big stories of those whom policy, timidity or cunning made "the brethren of the long bow." Authorized by the viceroy Mendoza to inquire into certain reports as to an alleged native empire to the northward Coronado swallowed with true Spanish gusto all the wonderful stories of the "Seven Cities of Cibola" that came to him. Here was a new Mexico to be conquered; here were wealth and empire to be had for the taking; he was to be a more successful Cortez, a richer Pizarro! He evidently essayed to investigate the reports with caution but he as evidently accepted as gospel all the crazy fictions of the crafty Indian, Tejos, all the pleasant fables of his own predecessor, Nuno de Guzman, all the incredible stories of that picturesque tramp Cabeza de Vaca, and all the barefaced falsehoods told by the monk Marcos, by the Munchasen-like negro Stephen and by that particularly mendacious native whom the "Conquerors" called "the Turk."

So, setting out from Compostella, the capital of his province, in the month of February, 1540, Coronado led into the northern wilderness a gallant array of gentlemen adventurers, sturdy fighters, and Indian allies.

Never were expectations more utterly blasted; never did high hopes go down in greater wreck. The expedition faced toward the north with the most glowing prospects of easy conquest and enormous booty. Across the desert the prize awaited them: "Seven great cities, the houses whereof were built of lime and stone, two, three, sometimes five stories in height, ascended on the outside by ladders; whose inhabitants clothed themselves in gowns of cotton, in woolen cloth, and in garments of leather, wearing girdles of turquoises around their waists, emeralds in their ears and noses; whose common household vessels were of gold and silver, and where gold was more abundant than in Peru, the walls of the temples being covered with plates of that precious metal."

Disappointment met them almost at the outset. But still they pressed on, lured by the promise that "just beyond" were the coveted treasures. "The seven cities of Cibola," says Mr. Skinner, "that reared themselves on the marge of Coronado's imagination as proudly as would Palmyra and old Tyre dwindled on his approach to ruined villages; nor could their occupants guide him to those veins and beds where precious stones and metals glistened and where they are to-day yielding up to our nation the wealth of an empire." The gold-seeking soldiers of Coronado daily spurned untold treasure beneath their feet and yet they knew it not.

Still on and on they pressed. Across the hills and valleys, the deserts, plains and water-courses of Arizona and New Mexico, penetrating, so it is claimed, even into the present confines of Colorado, of Kansas and Nebraska. Then they gave it up, and turning back retraced their homeward way a disappointed, dispirited and decimated band. Two years of wandering had yielded them neither empire, gold nor booty. Of all that gallant "army of conquest" only about an hundred tatterdemalions dragged themselves back to Mexico and all the brilliant visions of Coronado ended for him in defeat and disgrace. The viceroy Mendoza expended his wrath upon the unhappy leader, his governorship was taken from him and he himself died poor, forgotten, and half-crazed, the victim of a baseless dream of glory.

And yet Coronado deserved a better fate. He had but obeyed orders as a soldier should. He had found for civilization a land that was to be in time the treasure-house of the world; he had with admirable skill, as General Simpson now declares, led out an expedition that "for extent in distance traveled, duration in time and the multiplicity of its co-operating expeditions equalled, if it did not exceed, any land expedition that has been undertaken in modern times."

In how many instances the story of the *conquistador* was but a repetition of that of Coronado the musty pages of the old chroniclers, couched in crabbed Spanish or still more crabbed Latin, only too faithfully bear record. It was a time of rash endeavor, misty promise, and high expectation. Men risked their all for glory, for booty and for gold. Rumors were tortured into facts as across the broad Atlantic marvelous tales of still more marvelous regions reached the ears of European nations, already tingling, as Mr. Thompson says, " with the fascinating stories of Columbus and his followers. Mexico," he adds, " had fallen before Cortez; Peru had poured her spoils into the bloody hands of Pizarro. Ships were slipping away from the ports of Spain with their prows to the southwest. The wind in their sails was the breath of fortune. When the ships returned they came loaded down with gold and bearing the heroes of wild battles, the doers of strange deeds." What wonder that spendthrift hidalgoes with more pluck than possessions and avaricious dons, greedy for gold, should take a bond of fate in lands where glory and booty alike were to be won!

Such an one was the bankrupt farmer, Vasco Nunez called Balboa, who with an assurance that was almost monumental turned the contempt of his associates into confidence and forced their very waywardness to serve his private ends. Achieving advancement by energy he became successful both as conqueror and governor, coined the wealth of provinces into *castellanos* with which to line his own capacious pockets and became forever immortal as the discoverer of the vast Pacific.

Such, too, was Balboa's most relentless rival, Pedro Arias de Avila, known as Pedrarias, a sturdy fighter in the Moorish wars, but a man thoroughly wily, unscrupulous, politic, revengeful and vindictive. With him from San Lucar a gallant array of two thousand Spanish knights and gentlemen-adventurers went westward to the fairy-land of the Golden Castile where gems were as plentiful as Biscay herrings and gold was to be gathered from the ground in handfuls. It was a fatal harvest. Within one month after the landing at Darien seven hundred of that gallant following perished in the clutch of enemies more terrible than the infidel Moor — famine and disease. Disappointed, suspicious, passionate and envious Pedrarias vented his spleen upon his rival Balboa. He dispatched him on impossible missions, placed him in compromising situations and fairly forcing him into alleged treachery, brutally persecuted and finally killed the only man who could have helped him to the gold and the possessions he so greedily coveted.

Another such, swayed by the hope of gain, was the " Bachelor " Martin Fernandez de Enciso. Coming into the American provinces a speculative lawyer he turned the quarrels of men to his personal profit and accumulated by his successful law business a fortune of two thousand *castellanos* (about $11,000). Dazzled by the promise of the chief-justiceship of a conquered province he was tempted into investing his savings in a romantic venture and with strangely varying fortunes became in turn adventurer, soldier, conqueror, governor, rival, bankrupt, culprit and prisoner, as feud and faction tore asunder that struggling colony on the narrow Isthmus.

Such, too, were scores and hundreds of others — the dupes of false rumors, the sport of baseless promises. Led out by the hope of treasure and the possibility of rebuilding ruined fortunes they braved every danger and essayed the most reckless endeavors. The old records teem with their stories, compounded of mingled valor and rapacity, greed and bravery. Morales and the spoil of the Pearl Islands, Badajos and the gold of Parita, Gil Gonzales and the treasures of Nicaragua, Grijalva and the tribute of Vera Cruz, Guzman and the torture-wrung " presents " of New Galicia — the list could be extended for pages, fascinating as a romance of the paladins, repulsive in the realism of brutality, replete with heroism and suffering, treachery and cruelty, valor and strategy and the dash of daring deeds.

But always, in all this bravery, endurance and show of courage the deadly canker was at work — the greed for gold that, ever, with the *conquistador* went hand in hand with love of glory. Once again was the Scripture fulfilled: the love of money was, indeed, the root of all the evil that to this day has sullied the record of Spanish pluck and Spanish valor in America. It made of the cavalier a brute, of the knight a vulture, of the hidalgo a worse than murderer. It changed trusting natives into implacable foemen, it engendered hateful rivalries between leaders and turned the swords of comrades against one another's breasts.

It embittered the life of Columbus, wrecked the fame of Cortez and poisoned the glory of Alvarado. It did to death Balboa and Pizarro, Olid and Nicuesa, Garay and Ponce de Leon, Coronado and De Soto. It has linked with the memories of the boldest and bravest the never-dying scorn that a world, loving gain and gold, still visits upon the usurer, the extortioner and the assassin. It has capped the most marvelous of conquests with the greatest and basest of crimes.

While rightly the story of the old *conquistadores* belongs to the regions 'round about the Indies — to Mexico and the Antilles, to the Isthmus and the western coasts of South America — still, across the page of Northern story, falls the shadow of the Spanish warrior, defiant alike in exploration, in conquest and in defeat. The glitter of Spanish armor and the gleam of Spanish spur make picturesque the earlier annals of North American occupation when the golden banner of Spain floated above regions claimed for Cross and King beyond the Capes of Florida, on the shores of the Chesapeake and by the waters of the Hudson and the Mohawk. The iron heel of Spanish conquest left its enduring imprint upon lands that have for generations acknowledged occupation only by France or England and the colonizers of the seventeenth century found in the names that they presumed to be strictly Indian the traces of Spanish occupation and conquest of a far earlier day. But no one of these misty exploits rose to the importance or achieved the reputation of that wasteful, cruel, heroic and historic march made in the mid-years of the sixteenth century by De Soto and his men.

It is a stirring story and one that always bears retelling. Westward from San Lucar, that port of Seville from which had gone across the broad Atlantic so many ambitious cavaliers of Spain as full of hope, as certain of success as these, sailed Hernando de Soto and six hundred fighting men. Re-embarking at Havana, nearly a thousand strong, the expedition steered for its promised land and on the thirtieth of May, 1539, landed on the Florida coast, just east of the Everglades in that section of the State now known as Hillsborough Bay.

It was the most formidable expedition yet organized in America for conquest. Every man was a fighter; there were few gray hairs in the whole army, and at its head stood Hernando de Soto, one of the conquerors of Peru, a man amply qualified to lead a gallant host to victorious deeds. "In fame," says Dr. Monette, "he almost equalled the conquerors of Mexico and Peru themselves; in courage and perseverance he was not less. He was in the prime of manhood and only waited some fit opportunity to signalize himself and hand down his fame to posterity equally brilliant with that of Cortez and Pizarro."

Whatever was needful for an expedition of such magnitude was not lacking. There were wood-workers and iron-workers, there were chemists and miners, scholars and priests; there were tools for the builders, there was apparatus for assaying the "find" in gold and silver they were determined to obtain; there were chains and fetters for the captives, bloodhounds to pull them down, cards for the games of chance on which their captors might stake and hazard them. Nothing, it is asserted, was omitted from the "furniture" of the expedition "which experience could suggest or avarice and cruelty could dictate." The warm sun of Florida flashed down on the steel armor of the cavaliers glittering with gold; on coats of mail, on helmets, on breastplates and on shields; lance and broadsword, spear and cimeter gleamed in warlike hands; cross-bow and arquebuse rested upon many a stalwart shoulder and "stimulated by the love of fame and still more by the love of gold, this roving band of gallant freebooters plunged into the savage wilds" in which they expected to find empires more magnificent and treasure more abundant than their comrades had wrested from the conquered "emperors" of Mexico and Peru.

There was little at their landing-place on Hillsborough Bay to suggest treasure or empire. And from there even to the end the Spaniards were the dupes of the tribes they sought to conquer and did so cruelly maltreat. Grown wary through experience of the tortures of earlier white visitors — the credulous Ponce de Leon, the brutal Ayllon, the wretched Narvaez — the Florida Indians sought to rid themselves of these latest comers by alluring stories of great cities and vast treasures to the north or west — "just beyond!" So, "just beyond," this brilliant cavalcade was ever pushing, westward and yet further westward, growing each day less brilliant, each day more desperate. Through morass and swamp and dreary waste of sand, through tangled thicket and interminable forest, fording rivers, climbing mountains, fighting hostile hosts, always expectant, but with never a touch of the coveted gold, with never a sight of the gorgeous cities, they struggled on — a band of baffled marauders, grown more desperate with each day's disappointment, more cruel with each savage struggle for supremacy. For three weary years the zigzag hunt for fortune went slowly on. Up and down the land where perpetual summer reigns, over that section of our Southern country now known as the States of Florida, Georgia, Alabama, Mississippi, Louisiana and Arkansas they wandered on, a fellowship of valorous fighters vainly seeking for the impossible.

At last came the tragedy. One by one cavalier and artisan, spearman and priest dropped by

THE FIRST WHITE MAN

the way. The bones of their stern but gallant commander were lowered into their last resting-place, beneath the yellow waters of the mighty Mississippi; the wildernesses of the far Red River country forever dispelled the promise of gold or empire; and, with desire, effort and endurance alike dead within them, tattered, beggared, travel-worn and utterly disheartened, still fighting their inveterate Indian foemen till the hated land faded in the distance, they floated down the great river to the greater Gulf and to the ports of friendly Mexico — a miserable remnant of the gallant array of glittering cavaliers to whom San Lucar and Havana had bidden such hearty godspeed and farewell.

In all history there is scarcely to be found a sadder example of high hopes brought to ruin, of golden expectations unfulfilled. It is a story bright with heroic exploits, black with perfidious deeds. "The governor," says Orviedo, his chronicler, "was very fond of this sport of killing Indians;" and the marks of "the governor's sport" have streaked the winding trail of his wanderings with blood and left an irradicable stain upon his memory.

Brighter even than the story of Spanish heroism is the record of Indian patriotism. Step by step, through all these three years of wandering did the warlike tribes of the South, sinking their hereditary feuds, combine to repel the white invader. Stubbornly, tenaciously, heroically they contested the possession of their home-land and the bloody battle of Mauvilla, only saved to Spain by the charges of the resistless cavalry, proved the mettle, the valor and the self-devotion of the native American soldier.

What De Soto was, what were Ayllon and Guzman, Ojeda and Balboa, Ponce de Leon and de Cordova, Narvaez and Cabeza de Vaca, that, also, were the hundreds and thousands of others — fighting men and adventurers of every rank and of every grade in life — who essayed to win fame and fortune in the New World and who, because of their valiant and intrepid deeds, their heroic achievements and profitless accumulations, their high-sounding titles, and never-weakening bombast, their marches and their battles, their rivalries and their feuds, have ever been remembered under the name they coveted — *el conquistadores*, the conquerors.

With vast opportunities for bloodless and peaceable conquest, for Christian enlightenment and a gentler civilization they wrecked their mighty chances on the fatal reefs of greed. Never conquerors over themselves they have gone into history as destroyers and braggarts where they should have been upbuilders and gentlemen. The boast of one of them: "I am not merely a De Soto — though that, by St. James, were enough for any man. I am a Sotomayor, a Mendoza, a Bovadilla, a Losada, a — sir! I have blood royal in my veins, and you dare to refuse my challenge," was fitly answered by the response of a noble Englishman: "Richard Grenville can show quarterings, probably, against even Don Guzman Maria Magdalena Sotomayor de Soto, or against the bluest blood of Spain. But he can show, moreover, thank God, a reputation which raises him as much above the imputation of cowardice, as it does above that of discourtesy."

Still, with all their shortcomings — their vices, their cruelties, their greed, their bombast, their bigotries and their credulity the old *Conquistadores* were a valiant and picturesque lot. If their record is smirched with tyranny and their valor is dimmed with blood, their ancestry and environments may be proffered as at once the reason and the excuse. They were, at least, the first link in the chain of fighting men that joins the new America to the old and have therefore due claim to a prominent place in our story as typical of that savagely picturesque life, when as Maurice Thompson tells us "priests were pirates and gentlemen were robbers" — those romantic if brutal days when, according to Theodore Irving, "the knight-errantry of the Old World was carried into the depths of the American wilderness."

CHAPTER III.

COLONIAL FIGHTING-MEN.

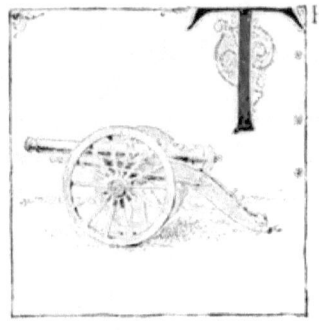

THE claim of Spain to the possession of the Western world was not long to remain undisputed. The audacious "Bull" of that Pope of Rome, Alexander VI., — who, himself a Spaniard and the favorer of his native land, sought to make all America Iberian — was a challenge to all the foes of Spain. And of these none were hotter, none more fierce than the daring spirits of England and of France.

At once ships and sailors, adventurers and fighters sailed over-sea in the very track of Columbus's caravels. Rivalries led to entanglements and these to relentless wars; and while those summer seas that men call the Spanish Main grew red with blood as Avarice grappled with Greed, and Spanish Bloodhounds snarled at English Mastiffs, still further to the north, in Canada and Virginia and along the Atlantic sea-board, the flags of France and England floated above struggling settlement and seaward-looking fort. After the first flush of disappointment at their failure to discover the always-coveted gold had passed the freebooter gave place to the trader; explorers became occupiers and adventurers settled down as colonists.

But, whether as adventurer, trader or colonist, life in the New World was ever precarious. To the danger of Indian attack and the personal jealousies of the settlers were added the race feuds, the religious differences and the international hostilities that made the American continent a continual battle-ground. For years one could scarcely dare assert what flag might on the morrow float above the colony of which he was a part. On the pine-fringed northern border Frenchman and Englishman struggled for the possession of Canada and with defensive fortresses fronted each other on the broken Maine coast. The valiant Champlain and the fiery Frontenac made for themselves glorious records as loyal captains of France and only the unyielding hostility of the warlike Iroquois kept them from the conquest of the English border-lands. Farther to the south Dutchman and Englishman quarreled as to the right of occupancy and colonization in the lands about the Connecticut and the Manhattans. Dutchman and Swede grappled over the problem as to which was to have and which to hold the banks of the Delaware. Rival English factions disputed over their rights on the Chesapeake and, to the still further south, first Spaniard and Frenchman and then Spaniard and Englishman fought for Florida and the Gulf, making the story of Southern occupation a fearful tragedy, stained with the blood of the victims of such a butcher as Menendez and the revenges of such an assassin as Gourges.

These continual disturbances, no less than the ever-present horrors of Indian hostilities, made every colonist of necessity a fighter. The trusty matchlock was as indispensable a piece of church equipment as psalter and prayer-book, and, after the stern manner of those days of trial, the stoutest arm and the sturdiest frame were the defense and stay of every settlement. The block-house and the palisaded fort were near at hand for convenient retreat and shelter, while every church that crested the hill-top was sanctuary and bristling arsenal as well.

Such a strong support — stout of arm and sturdy of frame — was that doughty Puritan fighter, Miles Standish, the Captain of Plymouth. Longfellow's portraiture might apply to many another hardy leader of the colonial fighting-men of those earlier days:

> "Short of stature he was, but strongly built and athletic,
> Broad in the shoulders, deep-chested, with muscles and sinews of iron;
> Brown as a nut was his face, but his russet beard was already
> Flaked with patches of snow, as hedges sometimes in November."

Many another, too, might be able to make his professional boast:

> "Look at these arms," he said, "the warlike weapons that hang here
> Burnished and bright and clean, as if for parade or inspection!
> So I take care of my arms as you of your pens and your inkhorn.
> Then, too, there are my soldiers, my great, invincible army,
> Twelve men, all equipped, having each his rest and his matchlock,
> Eighteen shillings a month, together with diet and pillage,
> And, like Cæsar, I know the name of each of my soldiers!
>
> Look! you can see from this window my brazen howitzer planted
> High on the roof of the church, a preacher who speaks to the purpose,
> Steady, straightforward, and strong, with irresistible logic,
> Orthodox, flashing conviction right into the hearts of the heathen.
> Let them come, if they like, and the sooner they try it the better, —
> Let them come, if they like, be it sagamore, sachem or pow-wow,
> Aspinet, Samoset, Corbitant, Squanto, or Tokamahamon!'"

As quick, as choleric and as impetuous, too, was many another Colonial captain, with just as peculiar and by no means kid-gloved methods of dealing with the Indian foeman. The stalwart Captain of Plymouth had little sympathy with the school of Las Casas and Eliot. Listen, as he sounds his defiance in the council:

> "What! do you mean to make war with milk and the water of roses?
> Is it to shoot red squirrels you have your howitzer planted
> There on the roof of the church, or is it to shoot red devils?
> Truly the only tongue that is understood by a savage
> Must be the tongue of fire that speaks from the mouth of the cannon!
>
> Leave this matter to me, for to me by right it pertaineth.
> War is a terrible trade; but in the cause that is righteous,
> Sweet is the smell of powder; and thus I answer the challenge!"
>
> Then from the rattlesnake's skin, with a sudden, contemptuous gesture,
> Jerking the Indian arrows, he filled it with powder and bullets
> Full to the very jaws, and handed it back to the savage,
> Saying, in thundering tones: "Here, take it! this is your answer!"

Such a fighter, though a much greater braggart, was Captain John Smith, the "paladin" of Virginia. Such, too, was Captain John Mason, of the Connecticut colony, victor in the Pequot War; and such were Captain Benjamin Church, the conqueror of "King" Philip, Captain "Nat" Bacon, the brilliant young Virginia fighter and leader in a somewhat remarkable rebellion, and Major Thomas Trueman, of Maryland, the murderer of the Susquehannoughs. Intrepid, deliberate and relentless, hating an Indian even more cordially than a "papist," their methods were short, sharp and decisive, and to their tactics and their peculiar plans of action is due, very largely, the heritage of the American nation in Indian hatreds and Indian wars.

Of all the fighting governors of colonial times Oglethorpe was the most heroic, Stuyvesant the most picturesque. Andros, with a full share of the belligerent spirit, was no match for a determined people; Berkeley, a type of the old-time tyrant, could have made no head against the patriotism of Bacon, had not death stepped in as his ally. Few, if any, of the royal governors, with the exception of Oglethorpe and Bienville, could suc-

THE REVOLT OF THE TRAIN-BANDS. "LEISLER, YOU MUST LEAD US!"

cessfully direct the war-spirit that slumbered in the breasts of colonial trader and husbandman. It needed the deeper and underlying home interests of native or naturalized governors to lead their neighbors to action and to victory. It was Leisler, of New York, the "people's governor," a captain in the city train-bands, who awakened in his fellow-countrymen the first desires for personal liberty and organized the first really offensive measures against the French power in Canada. It was Pepperell, the Maine merchant and militiaman, who at last brought this struggle for supremacy to a crisis and, conqueror of Louisburg, was the earliest of the native generals of his King.

For our present purpose it will be sufficient to give brief mention here to two of the colonial leaders — types of the foreign and the native stock — who developed the martial spirit in the people and made out of colonists and farmers the first real American soldiers. These shall be James Edward Oglethorpe and William Pepperell.

Born to a love of arms, a daring commander of men and a soldier of tried experience in European wars Oglethorpe yet came to the government of his Georgia colony desiring only peace, substantial growth and the good-will of men. That he was forced into prominence as a successful commander was due to the aggressions of the power of Spain.

Alarmed at the growth of English colonization in the South the Spanish rulers in Cuba and Florida determined to crush out the Saxon. Hostilities were not long in commencing. Frederica and Saint Augustine were not far apart and the Spanish attacks on the Georgia settlements were speedily followed by the English assault on the Florida fortress.

Oglethorpe was the soul of this latter movement. The friend of the Wesleys and of Whitfield and an ardent desirer of peace for his colony he was above all a soldier. If Spain determined for war, war she should have. His investment of St. Augustine was brilliant and strategic. Had he but been properly supported by his associates and subordinates the era of Spanish occupation in North America would have come to an end long before its lingering death nearly half a century later.

But though St. Augustine did not surrender Oglethorpe's energetic measures bore instant fruit. Men saw that the *aide-decamp* of Prince Eugene, the hero of Belgrade, had lost nothing of his old-time valor. Spain awoke to the fact that she must needs increase her power if she wished to overcome this old fighter of the Turks. Forced to the defensive until such time as they were able to prepare a strong and formidable armament the Spaniards for two years longer kept behind their stone walls. At last, in the summer of 1742, they gathered for the decisive blow. In that year this new Spanish Armada sailed from Havana well equipped for the final and utter extinction of the English power in the South.

But the spirit of his ancestors lived in the gallant Englishman. As the Oglethorpes of Surrey "in days of good Queen Bess" had rallied to the resistance of the first and greater Armada so he, too, determined upon an heroic stand. "If we have no succor," he wrote, "all we can do is to die bravely in His Majesty's service."

The Spanish fleet of fifty-one sail, carrying a force of nearly five thousand soldiers, bore down upon the Georgia coast. Oglethorpe had but six hundred and fifty men and a few small vessels. Men looked to see the Georgia colony go down in blood before the force of Spain.

But to a hero nothing is impossible. "With a bravery and dash almost beyond comprehension," says Mr. Jones, "by strategy most admirable, Oglethorpe by a masterly disposition of the troops at command, coupled with the timidity of the invaders and the dissensions which arose in their ranks, before the middle of July put the entire Spanish army and navy to flight."

His personal daring turned the battle of the Bloody Marsh from a rout to a victory; his inspiring courage beat back the Spanish galleys from an attack on Frederica and led the pursuit under the very guns of their war-ships; his pluck, his shrewdness and his ability to seize upon opportunities at just the right moment dismayed and confounded the Spanish commanders and absolutely drove away the invading army at the very instant when they might have struck a crippling blow and obtained a certain victory. There is much of truth, notwithstanding the apparent exaggeration, in Whitfield's enthusiastic comment: "The deliverance of Georgia from the Spaniards is such as cannot be paralleled but by some instances out of the Old Testament." And Mr. Lodge asserts that "Oglethorpe saved two provinces to England by as gallant fighting and shrewd generalship as the whole history of the American colonies can show. A brave soldier, an honest, upright, kind-hearted gentleman," so Mr. Lodge declares, "he is a man whom any State might regard with reverence and admiration as its founder, first ruler and defender."

Of a different character but no less the gentleman and the soldier was William Pepperell, the merchant of Portsmouth, in New Hampshire. A colonial shop-keeper with but little knowledge of war, honored and respected rather because of his thirty years of service as an upright judge and a successful political adviser than for his acquaintance with military needs and tactics Pepperell was placed in command of the land forces in New England's greatest crusade against Canada.

So skillfully did he conduct his part of the operations that the strong fortress of Louisburg on Cape Breton — the bulwark of Canada — fell after an almost bloodless siege of fifty days. "It was a gallant exploit," says Mr. Lodge, "almost the only glory of an unsuccessful war." The greatest triumph of colonial fighting-days was secured by an undisciplined army "of New England mechanics and farmers and fishermen" led on by a Yankee merchant.

It was really the first American army. Leisler's force of invasion, which a half-century before had failed through colonial jealousies and wrecked the mighty purpose of its energetic promoter, could scarcely assert its claim to be esteemed an American army. Pepperell's men were largely native-born. And William Pepperell, tradesman though he was, may safely be considered as the first native military leader produced by the colonies. Other commanders of American birth there had been but none had as yet been selected for so exalted a position. The titled adventurers who were royal governors by favor of the king of England were far too anxious themselves to pose as leaders and commanders to permit any mere "provincial" to usurp their dignities. It is therefore to the credit of Shirley, the King's Governor in Massachusetts and himself no mean soldier, that in the famous expedition against Louisburg he should have selected for chief command so able a native American as William Pepperell. This Canadian success led to immediate honors. The victorious commander was created Sir William Pepperell. He was acting governor of the colony of Massachusetts and in 1757 he was commissioned as lieutenant-general and commander of the Massachusetts militia, now grown to over seven thousand men. He died on the very eve of the victorious campaign that gave Canada to England.

Oglethorpe and Pepperell, however, were but the accompaniments and the outgrowth of the years that were opening

FRANKLIN AS A PRIVATE.

the way for the real American soldier. The hardships, the struggles, the defeats and the slow successes of colonial life brought to the service many leaders skilled in border war and toughened the temper of men from whom sturdy fighters came. Miles Standish's thirteen men, his "great, invincible army," could be duplicated in every one of the struggling settlements that looked out to the eastward upon the stormy Atlantic and westward into the no less dangerous wilderness. From these slender homeguards grew, in time, the provincial militia-men who volunteered for the wars against France and Spain and prepared the way for the greater revolution.

But not always in fighting Indians or invading hostile lands were the colonial fighting-men in arms. Too often were these arms turned against one another. In jealousies of office and in border disputes, in hair-brained endeavors and in open rebellion, time upon time, did brother face brother and neighbor neighbor in the hot encounters of those earliest days.

The very composition of the several colonies fomented discontent. The mixed character of the settlers aggravated disorder. From the time of beginnings, when Captain John Smith of the Virginia colony — "an adventurer of a high order in an age of adventurers" — came into direct conflict with Governor Wingfield and his other associates, down to that later day, when in Boston streets Crispus Attucks and his riotous companions faced, and fell before a platoon of British soldiers, dissatisfaction, jealousies, desire and unrest stirred up continual strife which not unfrequently blazed out into open rebellion. Chief among these popular uprisings, according to chronological order, were: the Ingle roysterings in Maryland in 1645, the Bacon rebellion in Virginia in 1675, the Culpepper revolt in North Carolina in 1677, the revolt of the people against aristocratic oppression in 1689 — led by Bradstreet in Massachusetts and Leisler in New York; the race "rebellion" of Father Sebastian Rasle in Maine in 1724, the election riots in Pennsylvania in 1739, the bloody march of the "Paxton Boys" on Philadelphia in 1763, and the revolt of the Regulators in South Carolina in 1764. The fight at Golden Hill, in New York City, and the Boston Massacre — both disturbances of the year 1770, and both rather vaingloriously claimed as "the first blood of the Revolution" — fitly closed an hundred and fifty years of struggle, sedition and dispute.

But, through all these (by means, even, of some of them) was the mixed condition of colonial society merging into something definite, into something American. As it took an hundred years and more to make of the caste-hedged emigrant of Europe a free American, so, too, did it need fully a century of emergencies to mold from the pioneer, the borderer and the partisan the real American soldier. For years the American colonist was but a transplanted Englishman, an expatriated Dutchman, an "assisted" German, Frenchman or Swede. These fought, when necessity compelled them, against Indian marauder or border enemy; they resisted, when personal grievances inflamed or local leaders urged them, the invasion of their assumed "rights," but they never marched, as Americans, step to step and shoulder to shoulder, until the final invasion of Canada and the first drum-beats of revolution cemented them together as Americans, as brothers conscious of their own strength and needs.

It was this lack of union that brought the rebellion of Bacon and the bold stand of Leisler to naught. And though each colony, as it grew in numbers and in strength, organized its able-bodied fighting-men into some semblance of a provincial militia, these "bulwarks of the state" did but little in the way of concerted action, and did that little grudgingly. It takes a great motive to change a partisan into a patriot.

As, around its church or block-house or ragged fort of logs, each struggling settlement grew, the earlier home-guards — which might be Captain Standish's

> "Twelve men, all equipped, having each his rest and his matchlock, Eighteen shillings a month, together with diet and pillage."

or might be the "three and fifty raw and tired Marylanders" whom "that noble, right valiant, and politic soldier" Thomas Cornwallis led against the Susquehannas — developed into the Train-Bands or Military-Bands common to each colony.

While from time to time the red-coat garrisons of the king became familiar sights in the larger towns, it was chiefly upon these Train-Bands, made up of their own numbers, that the people of the colonies depended for their military strength. "We know, from more than one incident," says Mr. Doyle, "that there was no lack of individual courage or soldierly skill among the settlers."

In every province the able-bodied male "freeholders" were held subject to military duty. When occasion demanded they could be called upon for active service. The charter of the Maryland province invested the proprietors with the right to "call out and arm the whole fighting population, wage war, take prisoners, and slay alien enemies; also to exercise martial law in case of insurrection." In Massachusetts each town, from the earliest days, had its own military company, for service in which every man was liable, excepting the "magistrates, elders, deacons, shipwrights, millers and fishermen."

The law of 1766 required all males in the colony to attend

military exercise and service. Each company of foot in the colonial militia was composed of musketeers and pikemen; two thirds bearing the matchlocks and the cumbersome "rest," one third carrying the long and murderous-looking pikes, or spears.

While the demands of farm and merchandise were held superior to those of war and while the colonist-soldier was ever slow to leave these until their protection became an absolute necessity the records of those old days show the train-band-man to have been an important factor in the life and growth of every settlement. "In the seventeenth century," says Mr. Lodge, "all men went armed; even the farmers wore swords, and the military spirit was wide-spread and ardent. All adults were in the militia and the training-day, when the soldiery went out to drill with pike and musket, was the great break in the dark monotony of daily life."

At the outbreak of the great English revolution of 1688 — a revolution that gave fresh impulse to the longings for personal liberty in America — the population of the colonies was less than two hundred thousand. Of this number perhaps thirty thousand may be considered a fair estimate for the fighting population — the persons able to bear arms. But of this latter estimate a small proportion only were really men-at-arms, members of the train-bands. Captain Underhill's "army," which, in 1640, at the instigation of the treacherous and bloody-minded Kieft he led out from Dutch New York against the defenseless Indians thereabouts, consisted of but one hundred and twenty men. The force at the head of which Captain John Mason, in 1637, marched from the Connecticut country to the extermination of the warlike Pequots was less than an hundred men. In 1675 the joint "army" of Massachusetts, Connecticut and Plymouth, raised under the spur of desperate necessity to fight the Indian warrior Philip of Pokanoket and drawn from a population of some seventy thousand souls, amounted to but eleven hundred men. The six free companies or train-bands of New York who in 1689, united under the energetic Leisler to strike if need be for the Stadtholder king and civil liberty numbered less than five hundred men; the whole provincial force that in that summer of 1689 responded to the summons of the first colonial congress and gathered on the northern frontier for the invasion of Canada fell far below the eight hundred and fifty men promised by the congress.

In fact, no considerable nor adequate military force was enlisted in the colonies for warlike purposes until the mid-years of the eighteenth century showed to England and her colonies, alike, that if America was to be the heritage of Englishmen the struggle with France must be a united one and fought to the bitter end. Then, at last, both king and colonist put forth their greatest strength. And in the seven years of war that broke the power of France in America and ended in triumph on the historic heights of Quebec no small share of the glory as of the fighting must be accorded to the now-aroused "provincials" whom British officers and soldiers so affected to despise.

This studied contempt of regulars for volunteers is but a part of the always-existing arrogance of military aristocracy. It held place in the legions of Rome as in the cohorts of Xerxes and reaches back even to that older day when by the Wells of Harod the chosen three hundred of Gideon lapped the water "like a dog" and were alone of all the Israelitish host, deemed worthy to fight the Midianites.

But never, surely, was there less reason for this professional bias than in the days of the colonial fighting-men of America.

It was the South Carolina militiamen who, rallying to the defense of their struggling colony in 1706, made so spirited an attack upon the French invaders that they drove back Le Feboure in defeat across Charleston bar with nearly one half of his eight hundred men killed or prisoners. It was the fifty Carolina volunteers of Governor Moore who, in 1702, plunged through the Georgia forests to the attack of the boastful Spaniards and established the claim of England to all the southern country as far as the walls of Saint Augustine. In the disastrous and horribly mismanaged expedition of 1739, by which England was to conquer the Spanish possessions of Mexico and Peru, it was the "provincials" who won the only fame that came from that ill-starred endeavor as, all unsupported, they led in the storming of the San Lazaro fortress of Carthagena; while of the thousands who left their bones in that pestilential climate nine tenths were the contemned "provincials." It was a New Hampshire volunteer, William Vaughn, who in the attack on Louisburg in 1745 — an enterprise in which, it is asserted, "the provincial forces displayed courage, activity and fortitude that would have distinguished veteran troops" — captured the royal French battery and with only thirteen men held it against all the enemy sent for its retaking. It was John Stark and his five hundred New Hampshire foresters who marched through the trackless wilderness that lay between the Connecticut and the Hudson, compassed the reduction of Crown Point and shed about the only light that fell upon the disgraceful defeat at Ticonderoga.

It was Phineas Lyman, the commander of the New England volunteers — "a man of uncommon martial endowments" — who, in 1755, won the victory at Lake George; and, on the same fatal day of Dieskau's defeat it was Macginnes and his two hundred provincials who met and thoroughly defeated a superior French force at the portage of Fort Edward. It was Benjamin Franklin of Pennsylvania, the father of the American militia (of whom Logan wrote: "I principally esteem Benjamin Franklin for saving the country by his contriving the militia"),

A MUSTER OF COLONIAL MILITIA ON BOSTON COMMON.

who, when elected in 1744 to the command of one of the regiments he had raised, declined the honor of leadership and himself marched in the ranks and did his sentry duty, carrying a musket as "a humble volunteer." It was Peyronney, the Virginia captain, who at Braddock's terrible defeat in 1755, "when those they call regulars ran like sheep before the hounds," still held the fight with his valiant colony men until he and nearly every man in his company were killed. It was George Washington the Virginia colonel ("that heroic youth," so wrote Davies, the New Jersey minister, "whom I cannot but hope Providence has preserved in so signal a manner for some important service to his country") who, on that same awful day, when the king's soldiers fell or fled before the Indian ambuscade, saved the rout from being an utter massacre; though shot at until two horses fell under him and his coat was riddled with bullets, he still protected the retreat, with what Braddock had contemptuously termed his "raw American militia." It was the men of Monckton's brigade — three out of every four of them being "provincials"— who stood the chief shock of the conflict on the Plains of Abraham where on "the battle-field of the Celtic and Saxon races" the valor of their stand gave victory to England in that one of the decisive battles of the world that closed the long struggle for supremacy in America with the death of the heroic but victorious Wolfe.

Of this final and greatest endeavor of the colonial fighting-men the story has become a twice-told tale. But it is worth relating here, as that of a struggle in which the undervalued "provincials" bravely bore their part and, waking to a sense of their real strength, made the Plains of Abraham but the forerunner of the yet grander plain known as the Common of Lexington.

The mid-years of the eighteenth century had come. For nearly an hundred and fifty years had England and France been crowding one another in the western world, each claiming its ownership, each determined to possess it. The success of England, though clearly foreshadowed, had not as yet been apparent. Canada might be doomed but France defended herself right valiantly. Louisburg had fallen. Acadia had been conquered, but to the northwest, above the rock-bound fortresses of Quebec and Montreal, the Bourbon banner of the *fleur-de-lis* still floated in triumph. France still held the key to the continent and in the great valleys of the west the blue uniforms of her guardsmen garrisoned all the rapidly-growing outposts.

The governors of New France were energetic and aggressive. To the grim and martial Frontenac had succeeded the politic De Callieres, the warlike Vaudreuil, the energetic Beauharnais, the wily Galissonière and La Jonquiere, admiral of France. Following him came, in turn, the impetuous Duquesne and yet another Vaudreuil — the last of the French governors. Equal in valor, though ever at odds with their official superiors, stood the royal commandants, than whom none were braver in fight than the last: Dieskau, who fell at Lake George, and Montcalm, the noble and heroic — Montcalm, whose career in Canada has been pronounced "a wonderful struggle against destiny."

England opposed but inferior leaders to these energetic sons of France. Braddock, the obstinate, fell in utter and almost ignominious defeat; Shirley and Johnston had neither the pluck nor the ability to follow up the advantages of success. Loudon was a pompous do-nothing, Abercrombie a slow and heavy-witted incapable, Amherst was a stolid and over-cautious martinet, Webb a timid and dilatory tactician. Only with Wolfe — young, brilliant, energetic and intrepid — did anything like real success come to the arms of England.

Sailing from conquered Louisburg, where his great ability had already displayed itself, Wolfe, in June, 1759, headed toward Quebec. The slow methods of England had enabled France to succor her principal stronghold in Canada and when Wolfe landed on the Island of Orleans Amherst's twelve thousand men still lingered on the shores of Lake Champlain. "The whole mass of the people of Canada," says Bancroft, "had been called to arms," and Wolfe, with his less than eight thousand men, found himself fronted by Montcalm with a force of fourteen thousand, not counting the Indian allies." The entire summer was wasted in ineffectual attempts on either side to obtain the advantage; Amherst and his expected reinforcements did not appear and at last on the third of September Wolfe decided upon a movement as adventurous as it was hazardous.

Sick in body but intrepid in spirit he ordered his men to scale the precipitous heights above Quebec. Here was the one weak point of the enemy; here must the assault be made. Once determined upon this was quickly done. Aided by "sheer good luck quite as much as by skill and courage" Wolfe and his little force — exactly four thousand eight hundred and twenty-six in number — in the gray of a September morning, silently pulled themselves up the steep incline and at sunrise, says Mr. Clinton, "looked down from the Heights of Abraham upon the city which for nearly three months they had wearily watched across the water."

Thus outgeneraled and surprised Montcalm saw that instant action was his only salvation. With his seventy-five hundred fighting men he marched to meet the enemy. The battle was joined at once. On came the French; but not until they were within forty yards of the "thin red line" of England was their fire returned. Then the iron hail burst from the English ranks; another volley quickly followed and, as the smoke cleared away, Wolfe charged the wavering French line. The blue coats broke in panic; alike English and French commander fell mortally wounded and as the French battalions turned in flight the fate of Canada was sealed. One of the decisive battles of the world was fought and won in precisely ten minutes by the watch.

Montreal fell in the following summer. Rogers and his American rangers captured the western posts and with the close of 1760 the last hope of France was extinguished. The lilies of the French king fell in surrender; the red cross of St. George waved over conquered fortresses and captured posts, and America was English from the St. Lawrence to the Gulf.

The thirteen colonies were wild with joy. They were saved. The always-present danger of French conquest was over forever and its final overthrow was due as much to American valor as to English discipline. Though British councillors and commanders might sniff and sneer, the people knew in how great measure they had helped to the end. "Provincials," says Bancroft, "had saved the remnants of Braddock's army; provincials had conquered Acadia; provincials had defeated Dieskau." And provincials, too, had captured invulnerable Louisburg, had destroyed Fort Frontenac, reduced Niagara and planted the English flag in victory on the ruined bastions of Duquesne.

Such a schooling in warfare as that was not to go unheeded. Alike ranger and forester, militiaman and volunteer gained the inspiration of victory from this, the last stand against France. The day for yet greater deeds was close at hand and the colonial fighting-man was to become the defender and the deliverer of his home-land. English contempt was to develop into English tyranny and at the call of their leaders the despised provincials of the past were to become the patriots of the future. From the ranks of the village train-bands and the colonial militiamen was to step ready and armed for resistance the determined and now immortal Minute-man. The real American soldier was ready at last.

CHAPTER IV.

MINUTE-MEN AND CONTINENTALS.

MR. BRATTLE presents his Duty to his Excellency Gov. Gage, he apprehends it his Duty to acquaint his Excellency from Time to Time with every Thing he hears and knows to be true and is of Importance in these troublesome Times, which is the Apology Mr. Brattle makes for troubling the General with this Letter, Capt. Minot of Concord, a very worthy Man, this Minute informed Mr. Brattle that there had been repeatedly made pressing Applications to him to warn his Company to meet at One Minutes Warning, equipt with Arms and Ammunition, according to Law; he had constantly denied them, adding, if he did not gratify them he should be constrained to quit his Farms and Town; Mr. Brattle told him he had better do that than lose his Life and be hanged for a Rebel."

Thus, on the twenty-ninth of August, 1774, ran the opening

of a letter addressed to the commanding officer of the British troops in Boston by William Brattle, the brigadier in command of the provincial militia. For Boston was garrisoned by the troops of King George. The temper of her people was hot and aggressive toward England and the authorities across the water had determined to nip rebellion in the bud.

It was a note of warning, but it came too late. Military rule in America meant an increase of oppression; and to further oppression men were unalterably opposed. Resistance was duty. To this duty the colonists were urged and those especially who enrolled in the militia were implored to hold themselves ready for any emergency. And at last the emergency came.

For years the relations between king and colonists had been growing more and more strained. Freedom from absolute influence of the kingly authority had for more than a generation been creating in men a desire for greater personal freedom. There is a mighty impetus toward emancipation in the un-bridged distance of three thousand miles of sea.

So at last out of dispute came action. Tyranny on the one side and unyielding opposition on the other ended as it only could end — in blows, and when the clash came the "minute's warning" had its full effect. The Minute-men were ready and alert.

The first shock of arms came in the Massachusetts colony. When the British government sent orders to General Gage, the commander in Boston, that he should bid his troops fire upon the people when he should deem it necessary, the match was put to the tinder. The people's protest showed itself in the storing of munitions of war for their own defense and in the drill and continual readiness of the Minute-men. In 1775 came the climax.

"On the nineteenth day of April, one thousand seven hundred and seventy-five, a day to be remembered by all Americans of the present generation, and which ought and doubtless will be handed down to ages yet unborn, the troops of Britain, unprovoked, shed the blood of sundry of the loyal American subjects of the British king in the field of Lexington." So ran what Dr. Hale calls "the prophetic introduction" of the report of the Battle of Lexington which the provincial congress of Massachusetts forwarded in haste to England.

Of that notable nineteenth of April how often has the story been told. And yet, who tires of reading it? From the instant when Paul Revere caught the flash of the signal lantern from the pigeon-haunted belfry of the North Church in Boston town and rode his ride of warning the story grows in interest.

> "And lo! as he looks, on the belfry's height
> A glimmer and then a gleam of light!
> He springs to the saddle, the bridle he turns,
> But lingers and gazes, till full on his sight
> A second lamp in the belfry burns!
> A hurry of hoofs in a village street,
> A shape in the moonlight, a bulk in the dark,
> And beneath, from the pebbles, in passing, a spark
> Struck out by a steed flying fearless and fleet:
> That was all! And yet, through the gloom and the light,
> The fate of a nation was riding that night;
> And the spark struck out by the steed in his flight,
> Kindled the land into flame with its heat."

The land was ready to be kindled. The anxious waiting of Paul Revere as, all

> "impatient to mount and ride
> Booted and spurred, with a heavy stride,"

he paced the grassy shore of the "sluggish Charles" was but typical of the unsettled feeling that pervaded all the colonies. Not alone in Massachusetts were bold men urging action. North and south the mysterious "Sons of Liberty" were forming. In more than one section were to be found those who expressed not only their willingness but their desire to fight.

From that historic seventh of October, 1765, when in the city of New York, a congress of the thirteen colonies voiced the protest of the people against the tyranny of England down to the climax-year that precipitated revolution, the people were everywhere preparing. The spirit of resistance broke out again and again. The angry crowd that danced about the effigy of Oliver the stamp-master, as it dangled from a Boston elm, the five hundred hard riders who stopped the way of Ingersoll the Connecticut collector and forced him to resign his office, fling aloft his hat and hurrah three times for "Liberty and Property," the New York mob that broke open the stables of the royal governor, dragged out his coach, mounted his Excellency's effigy upon it and then burned the whole equipage on the Bowling Green, the four hundred Marylanders who assembled at Frederick town armed with "guns and tomahawks" and threatened to break up the provincial government, the indignant people of North Carolina who threatened the British war-sloop that bore the stamped paper, seized its boat, which they dragged on a cart to Wilmington and there surrounding the governor's house threatened to burn both house and governor if he did not accede to their demands, the mutterings of opposition in Pennsylvania, in South Carolina and in Georgia that rose and fell with popular opinion and were displayed in the customary mobs and effigy burnings — all these were but the precursors of that determined opposition to tyranny that, after ten years of smouldering, was fanned into a flame by the famous stand of the Minute-men on Lexington Common and about the old North Bridge at Concord — the historic span of America's Rubicon, the sacred spot

> "Where once the embattled farmers stood
> And fired the shot heard round the world."

It was that day's fight that showed the courage and tested the spirit of America's citizen soldiery.

Little need to tell here the story of Lexington. Every school-boy is familiar with its details and not a few schoolboys of that distant day seemed to have been filled with prophetic inspirations. It is related that as Lord Percy's troops marched out of Boston heading for the highway that led toward distant Concord they played with much spirit the shrill but sarcastic strains of Yankee Doodle. "Ho, ho!"

"THEY HUNG ON THE SKIRTS OF THE RETREAT."

jeeringly called out a smart Roxbury boy perched on a convenient stone wall, "you fellows go out by 'Yankee Doodle;' you'll come back fast enough by 'Chevy Chase.'"

And a "Chevy Chase" it was indeed. The Percy of that famous day essayed the role of his ancestor of three centuries back only to repeat on Massachusetts highways the story of that "woful hunting" in Scottish woods. The old ballad tells us how

> "To drive the deer with hound and horn
> Earl Percy took his way;
> The child may rue that is unborn
> The hunting of that day."

The "embattled farmers" of the fair New England fields like the supporters of another Douglas rallied to protect their homelands and by their acts said as did he

> "Show me," said he, "whose men you be
> That hunt so boldly here,
> That, without my consent, do chase
> And kill my fallow-deer?"

The Minute-men won the day. Baffled and dispirited the British marauders straggled back to Boston. Like bull-dogs the now aroused farmers snapped and growled at their heels; they hung on the skirts of the retreat; with flint-lock and king's-arm they emphasized their protests and only desisted when the British troops were safe again beneath the protecting batteries of Boston town.

Here was war at last. The tidings of that long day's fight fired the colonies from Maine to Georgia. North, west and south the stirring tidings sped. It was on Wednesday the nineteenth of April, 1775, that Lord Percy's routed columns ran their twenty-mile race with death. On Sunday morning following, a swift courier clattered down the Broad Way bringing the story of the fight to New York. Elizabeth, New Brunswick, Princeton, Philadelphia, quickly heard the news. On the twenty-seventh it was in Baltimore and in the early days of May the southern colonies knew of the bravery of the Massachusetts farmers and cheered the tidings lustily. The Minutemen of the old Bay colony had precipitated revolution.

On that very tenth of May when the men of Georgetown in South Carolina flung aloft their caps at the news of Lexington fight, away to the North, amid the rolling hills that make so picturesque the verdant shores of Lake Champlain, another body of New England Minute-men, gathered from among the New Hampshire Grants and known as the Green Mountain Boys, made a dash upon the enemy that has become famous in history.

Led on by Ethan Allen, a mountain partisan, and Benedict Arnold, a Connecticut horse-jockey, less than an hundred Green Mountain Boys surprised the British post of Ticonderoga in the early dawn of that May morning. Thus unceremoniously routed from his bed, the sleepy commandant had the distinction of making the first actual surrender of the king's property to the revolting colonists, yielding with as good grace as possible to the rather pompous summons of the blustering Allen who summoned him to surrender the fort " in the name of the Great Jehovah and the Continental Congress!"

" The careful annalists," says Dr. Hale, "observe that the Continental Congress did not meet until after the surrender of Ticonderoga." But little did Allen care. He had a point to make and he made it. No one comprehended better than did this bold borderer the force of the questionable old adage: "All is fair in love and war."

Lexington and Ticonderoga were but the awakening. Minute-man and militiaman, responding to the call of the Committee of Safety, hurried to the investment of Boston. They had whipped the British in the open field; now they would push them into the ocean.

Mr. Frothingham has a story to the effect that when on one of those last days of May, 1775, the British generals, Howe,

Clinton and Burgoyne, were sailing into Boston harbor with reinforcements for the army of the king, they spoke a packet, outward-bound. Burgoyne hailed the skipper: "What news above?" he cried. Back came the answer that Boston town was surrounded by ten thousand countrymen. "How many

GREEN MOUNTAIN BOYS ON THE MARCH.

regulars in Boston?" asked the Englishman. "About five thousand." "What!" shouted Burgoyne, "can ten thousand Yankee Doodles shut up five thousand soldiers of the king? Well; well! Only let us get in there and we'll soon find elbow-room."

But that elbow-room never came. Closer and tighter about the beleaguered town drew the cordon of besieging yeomanry. In all the country 'round farmers and village folk grasped musket and pikes ready for action, and hurried to the places of rendezvous — and on the seventeenth of June the Provincial Congress, assembled at Watertown, issued an order that ran as follows :

"WHEREAS the hostile Incursions this Country is exposed to, and the frequent Alarms we may expect from the Military Operations of our Enemies, make it necessary that the good People of this Colony be on their Guard and prepared at all Times to resist their Attacks, and to aid and assist their Brethren: Therefore, *Resolved*, That it be and hereby is recommended to the Militia in all Parts of this Colony, to hold themselves in Readiness to march at A MINUTE'S WARNING, to the Relief of any Place that may be attacked, or to the Support of our Army, with at least twenty Cartridges or rounds of Powder and Ball. And, to prevent all Confusion or Delays, It is further recommended to the Inhabitants of this Colony, living on the Seacoasts, or within twenty Miles of them, that they carry their Arms and Ammunition with them to Meeting, on the Sabbath and other Days, when they meet for public Worship."

Summons and caution came none too soon. On that very seventeenth of June the environed British made one bold push for release. Their jailers were prepared for them. The battle of Bunker Hill was fought.

It proved the sturdiness as it tested the courage of the American Minute-man. A moral victory although an actual defeat, the battle of Bunker Hill showed alike to English soldier and to Colonial tory that Boston-town was not to be held in safety for the king.

On the same historic seventeenth of June the Continental Congress, in session at Philadelphia, appointed as "generalissimo" of the soldiers of revolt, Colonel George Washington of Virginia. Fighting men from all the New England colonies, volunteers from the middle provinces, riflemen from Maryland and Virginia and the further south, led by their own officers

THE MINUTE-MEN.

and making in all a loosely-organized force of more than sixteen thousand men, encamped upon the hills and plains to the west of Boston.

Under a spreading elm on the commons of Cambridge — a tree that yet stands, strong and sturdy, the best memorial of that time of blossoming revolution — minute-men and riflemen, militiamen and volunteers were mustered on the third of July, 1775; and there "His Excellency George Washington, Esquire, Captain-General and Commander-in-Chief of the Forces of the Thirteen United Colonies" assumed command of the soldiers of freedom. Revolution was organized. The Minute-men of Lexington and Bunker Hill became from that day forward the Continental Army.

But, before we turn from this opening chapter in the real story of the American soldier, let us glance at those historic figures that, by their deeds, so royally illustrate its pages. These Minute-men, this raw militia, that faced and fought the well-trained red-coats of England — who were they? What were they like?

Soldiers we can scarcely call them, for the soldier presupposes discipline, drilling and training. Some crude instruction of this sort they may have had. Some of the men, indeed, were veterans of the colonial conflicts that had preceded the Revolution, but as a rule these first fighters for liberty were busy toilers all, farm-born or village bred. Hastily summoned and still more hastily accoutered they left the plough in the furrow, the tool on the bench, the quill in the ink and, all unused to war, sprang to arms. In motley uniforms, in half-uniforms, in no uniform at all, with here a military coat, there a three-cornered hat or perhaps only a home-made cockade pinned to the homespun lapels, with the rusty flint-lock caught down from above the broad chimney-piece where it had hung for years as heirloom or trophy, a motley array, lacking in discipline, over-generous of advice to their superiors — neighbors, comrades and brothers all, they had swarmed to the ragged fences that flanked the king's highway between Concord and Boston; they had camped in most unmilitary style on hillside or in field, fallen behind the hastily-tossed earthworks on Bunker Hill or died beneath the blossoming apple-trees beside the flowing Mystic.

And the officers about whom these earlier fighters rallied were a scarcely less motley group than were the men who but haltingly acknowledged their authority. Here in the first fights for freedom, within the straggling camps or meeting in that first council of war at the foot of pleasant Prospect Hill came the waverer, the blusterer, the man of moderate experience, the would-be martinet, the newly-elected captain, ignorant of tactics and uncertain as to the proper use of his sword — food for merriment and contempt among the trained warriors of the English king, but patriotic none the less, formidable because sheathed in the justice of their cause.

> "Thrice is he armed that hath his quarrel just;
> And he but naked, though locked up in steel,
> Whose conscience with injustice is corrupted" —

Surely never did those noble words which the great poet puts into the mouth of an English king find fitter application than toward these patriot leaders in the new England across the seas, where once again the old issue between tyranny and personal freedom was to be fought to the end.

Here, to the leadership at the camp on Prospect Hill, came Heath the only colonel or, at least, the first of the colonels;

here, too, came Artemas Ward, "commander-in-chief" by
sufferance; Prescott of Pepperell, the valiant veteran of the
Canadian campaign; Putnam, the modern Cincinnatus, who
literally turned from the plough to the battle-field; Warren the
Roxbury doctor and busy committee-man, who fought as a
volunteer and fell in the rush from the captured earthworks,
the noblest victim of the stand on Bunker Hill; Knowlton
the brave Connecticut leader; Gridley the cannonier who had
trained the guns on Louisburg; Stark the doughty Indian
fighter from the New Hampshire Grants and Reed the equally
intrepid son of those granite hills; Brooks, the Medford major;
Thomas the Kingston doctor; Spencer of Connecticut; Greene
of Rhode Island — men whose names are indissolubly linked
to those opening days of revolution and whose memories
should linger with their countrymen as of those who by
their courage, their endurance and their sturdy patriotism fired
and cemented the stock from which was to spring the real
American soldier.

"Will he fight?" asked General Gage, as, in the battery on
Copp's Hill the tory lawyer who stood by the General's side
pointed out the stalwart figure of his rebel brother-in-law,
rallying the farmers behind the rudely-lined breastworks on
Bunker Hill.

"Fight!" was the reply, "yes, yes; you may depend on him
to do that to the very last drop of blood in his veins."

A notable figure in those stirring days was this same rebel
brother-in-law Colonel William Prescott. A type of the American fighters for freedom, his statue to-day fitly crowns the
height which he so valiantly defended and seems to guard the
tall gray shaft that commemorates for us that eventful seventeenth of June. Fifty years of age, a splendid figure, handsome

of face, full of energy and of inspiring words, he wore that hot June day in the trenches a simple uniform — the blue coat, lapped and faced and adorned with a single row of buttons; the knee breeches and silver-buckled shoes, and the inevitable three-cornered hat, while his directing hand grasped the unsheathed sword whose temper had already been proven in battle for that English king who was now no longer his master.

Of a like type and of equal valor were the men who commanded and the men who followed, the men who fought and those who fell in the opening battles of the war.

It was these fighters from the New England farms and their brethren from the plantations of the further South — frank, fearless, illy-disciplined, determined and alert, who gathered on the commons of Cambridge and, merging themselves into the Continental Army, accepted George Washington of Virginia as their commander and generalissimo.

Such then, when he took command at Cambridge, were the troops of Washington. "A hardy militia, brave and patriotic, but illy-armed, undisciplined, unorganized and wanting in almost everything necessary for successful war."

What could he make of them?

Full justice can never be done to the ability of the first American General. Hampered and harassed by the uncertainty of his forces, by the lack of proper munitions of war, by the half-hearted measures of a hesitating Congress and even by the wavering desires of the people whose interests he was to defend, he was yet able, with all the hazards against him, to drive a disciplined British Army from Boston and to hold against gathering odds the important city of New York. Defeated at Brooklyn by a force of British regulars outnumbering him three to one, he saved his army by one of the most mas-

"THE BRITISH ARE COMING."

terly retreats known to history. With forces continually decimated by desertions and by the unceremonious leave-taking of militiamen whose short terms of service were constantly expiring, he yet so maneuvered, marched and handled his disheartened forces as to strike, at just the critical moment, at the very center of Britain's chief dependence — the hireling Hessians at Trenton. And thus he grasped out of almost certain defeat the victory that strengthened the patriotic cause and resulted finally in the one measure that he knew was necessary for success — the organization and establishment of a regular army.

America's merriest Christmas was, really, the one that promised to be its sorriest — that eventful twenty-fifth of December, 1776, when Washington's meagre force pushed through the floating ice of the Delaware and captured the unsuspecting Hessians. "The life of a nation," says Mr. Lodge, "was at stake." Washington's brief campaign at Trenton and at Princeton has rightly been characterized as quite as brilliant and as full of skill and daring as is anything in the annals of modern warfare. Mr. Lodge asserts that, if Washington had never fought another battle, this decisive action on the Delaware would entitle him to the place of a great commander.

That it was decisive no one who reads history carefully can question. It reassured a doubting nation, organized strength out of weakness, brought triumph from disaster and, as one of its immediate results, merged all the shifting forces of the unreliable Continentals into the definite and finally victorious army of the Soldiers of Liberty.

That brief period from the muster beneath the elms of Cambridge Common in the warm July weather of 1775 to the cold

Christmas night on the Delaware in the dying days of 1776 is crowded with incident. It saw the disastrous invasion of Canada that ended in defeat at Montreal and Quebec; the death of the gallant Montgomery, one of America's most promising generals, and the daring of Arnold whose later treason, even, should not be permitted to eclipse his brilliant record amid Canadian snows. It saw the patriot victories in North Carolina; the

THE CAMBRIDGE ELM.

gallant defense of Charleston by the heroic Moultrie; the stubborn but hopeless effort to hold New York, the remarkable battle of Brooklyn, the spirited engagements at Harlem Heights and White Plains. It brought to the front men whose names were to become famous as intrepid and gallant fighters; and, through the inefficiency of British generals and the tireless labors of Washington drew to what was in fact, if we regard the numbers engaged, but a trifling military campaign the attention and the plaudits of a watching world.

A large, a veteran and a disciplined army, led by generals whom England esteemed her best, was out-maneuvered by a demoralized assemblage of untried and unreliable militiamen, "not much superior," says General Cullom, "to an armed mob;"

but the one was held together by a machine-like discipline and backed by an obstinate tyranny, the other, unsatisfactory though it might be, was still inspired by a determined patriotism. When disaster seemed most certain triumph came forth, and out of the most unpromising surroundings there emerged, to carry the war to its close, the dauntless Soldiers of Liberty. Henceforward minute-man, militiaman and continental are to stand through all that struggle for freedom as the veteran American Soldier.

CHAPTER V.

SOLDIERS OF LIBERTY.

"SIR, the Hessians have surrendered!" Thus, in joyful tones, came Baylor's report as, in a lull in that sharp morning's fight at Trenton, he galloped up to the anxious Commander-in-Chief.

"Thank God!" was Washington's devout rejoinder. And that fervent exclamation of gratitude, the simplest and yet the strongest that man can utter, was freighted with a still deeper meaning than even Washington himself could imagine. For that triumphant report of the hard-riding Baylor bore in its one brief sentence the success of the Revolution.

It is always darkest just before the dawn. When Glover's fishermen-soldiers from Marblehead, on that cold December night of 1776, pushed out into the floating ice the clumsy boats that were to carry Washington's troops across the Delaware the expedition seemed to be but a forlorn hope.

The little force of twenty-five hundred men, whose ill-shod

feet had literally marked their march across the snow with blood, constituted almost the entire fighting force at Washington's disposal. His army had, as yet, no compelling law to hold its numbers intact or keep its volunteers reliable. Here to-day and gone to-morrow seemed to be the rule with the home-raised militia who had ranged themselves under his banner.

Something must be done. The more than thirty thousand men who made up the British Army about New York so far outnumbered the Continental fighting-force that could be counted on for actual service that ruin to the patriot cause seemed almost inevitable. But despair formed no part of Washington's indomitable nature. Success must be won. In the most somber of those dark days he wrote to his brother, "I cannot entertain the idea that our cause will finally sink though it may remain for some time under a cloud."

And it was from under this cloud that he determined to bring the cause that was dearer to him than life. When, erect but anxious, he directed from his open flat-boat the crossing of his little army from one icy bank to the other he literally, as Mr. Lodge asserts, "carried the American Revolution in his hands." This one stroke of Washington's generalship saved the cause of the colonies. For, apart from the moral effect of the victory, it aroused a hesitating Congress to agree to Washington's demand for a standing army.

The enthusiasm that blazes into conflict and breaks into open rebellion against tyranny not unfrequently fails to stand the test of prolonged endeavor when the first frenzy of indignation is past.

To a certain extent this was true of the American revolutionists. The valor that lined the fences and thronged the fields between Concord and Boston, that led the assault on

Ticonderoga and held the breastworks on Bunker Hill grew lukewarm with long days of inaction in camp. Crops were growing in the home farm-lands; work which seemed quite as important as forcing the English king to yield to colonial demands had been left to over-burdened housewives or to unskilled helpers. When their brief term of enlistments came to an end the volunteers were quite ready to hurry back to their crops, their stock or their neglected duties at home.

So, again and again, the militia of the land, who acknowledged no central authority and were held only by their pledges to a short term of actual service would dwindle to a mere handful or be succeeded by raw levies who must be schooled to the demands and discipline of warfare.

In a letter to the President of the congress, written after the defeat on Long Island and that masterly retreat from Brooklyn, Washington said: "The jealousy of a standing army and the evils to be apprehended from one are remote and in my judgment, situated and circumstanced as we are, not at all to be dreaded; but the consequence of wanting one according to my ideas formed from the present view of things, is certain and inevitable ruin. For, if I was called upon to declare upon oath whether the militia have been most serviceable or hurtful, upon the whole, I should subscribe to the latter."

He had his wish at last. On the twenty-seventh of December, 1776, the very day after the brilliant dash upon the Hessians at Trenton, Congress "having maturely considered the present crisis and having perfect reliance on the wisdom, vigor and uprightness of General Washington," granted him the power as General of the United States to raise, organize and officer sixteen battalions of infantry, three thousand light-horsemen, three regiments of artillery and a corps of engineers.

This was to be considered as in addition to the eighty-eight battalions furnished by the separate States.

Here was high-sounding promise indeed, but it was never fully realized. It accomplished one excellent result, however, for it paved the way for the attainment of Washington's desires. For, though the numbers obtained were far too few for the always pressing needs of the revolted colonies and though the promises of the States were but meagerly fulfilled, a plan of enlistments for the term of at least three years kept up a standing force throughout the rest of the revolution. This supplied a basis on which Washington as commander-in-chief could frame his campaigns; while the militia, called out for extra service when occasion demanded, enabled the Congress to keep a fair showing of a fighting-force always in the field.

And yet, correct as was Washington's judgment and uncertain as was this fluctuating militia, how often upon their action did victory depend? It was the minute-men and militia of New England who gave the lie to the assertion of the bullying peers of Britain that the Americans would not fight. Before the guns of these same hastily-gathered militia-men the very flower of the British army reeled backward down the smoke-wreathed slope of Bunker Hill. It was the militia of the Mohawk Valley who stood the brunt of the bloody battle of Oriskany. It was the militia of New Hampshire and New York who stormed the earthworks at Bennington, captured or scattered the Hessian foeman and saved Mollie Stark from widowhood. It was the militia who triumphed over Burgoyne at Saratoga, decided the fate of the Revolution and made that famous engagement one of the fifteen decisive battles of the world. It was the militia of the South — the men who marched with Pickens at Charleston, with Campbell and Sevier at King's

Mountain, with Stephens at Guilford and with Marion at Eutaw —who came to the assistance of the regular Continental troops and, again and again, turned defeat into victory.

It is in no part the province of this volume to describe in detail the battles of the Revolution. Our duty lies rather in photographing, as well as we are able, the American Soldier who fought for the liberty of his land. The story of the several engagements that begun at Lexington and ended at Yorktown has been so often told and re-told that to give it space here would be but rehearsing a many-times told tale.

But every new battle, whether it ended in defeat or victory, made the American fighter still more a soldier and ever from the despair of the moment sprang a hope for the future. In whatever part of the country the tramp of British regulars startled the timid and angered the brave, the demand for immediate action brought a ready response. From farm and shop, from village and from clearing came the excited yeomanry hurrying to the support of the harassed Continentals.

The very lack of any distinctive uniform among those hastily-gathered recruits served a double purpose, in that it was at once a test of their patriotism and a blind to the enemy.

When, at Bennington, the aroused New England farmers answered the summons of the gallant Stark and encompassed the rear of Baum's heavily-armed Hessians the very manner of their coming disarmed suspicion. The detested foreigners were all regulars, "picked," says Mr. Fiske, "from the bravest of the troops which Ferdinand of Brunswick had led to victory at Creveld and Minden." What could a force of unskilled countrymen do against this historic prowess? And yet Yankee shrewdness overmatched German tactics. Stealthily and leisurely, almost as if seeking protection, the little squads of farmers, dressed in their long blue frocks and not over a dozen in a company, hung on the flanks of the German invaders or strolled carelessly to the rear. Good General Baum, a veteran of the stately European battle-fields counted these stragglers as nothing more than the Tory farmers whom he had

THE BATTLE OF ORISKANY.

expected to come within his lines, seeking protection from their rebel neighbors. But, ere the sun set, Bennington saw another sight. For when the Indian fighter Stark, at the head of five hundred militia, boldly charged the Hessians in front, these groups of supposed Tory farmers, now grown to five hundred or more, levelled their muskets at the King's troops and, from rear and flank, poured in a murderous fire. Thus was Bennington made a victory for the Colonists.

In like manner, of the forty-eight hundred men who rallied around Washington and, on the field of Princeton faced the veterans troops of England, more than three fifths were merchants, mechanics and farmers, ignorant of war. Inspired by the daring dash on the Hessian force at Trenton they had rushed from their homes, careless of mid-winter cold and full of the hope that, after all, the liberty they had begun to despair of was not impossible.

When, upon what was at that day the very outskirts of civilization, St. Leger and his motley array of seventeen hundred mingled British, Tories and Indians, tramped into the Mohawk Valley, it was the eight hundred and more Dutchmen of that western frontier who rallied to the call of heroic old Herkimer and, amid the pelting rush of one of August's fiercest thunder-storms, fought and won the battle of Oriskany — "the bloodiest and most picturesque battle of the Revolution."

When, later, the pompous declaration of Burgoyne that, with ten thousand men, he could promenade through America, ended in utter disaster at Saratoga, it was the supporting farmers from the country round and from the distant New England hills who fought that "battle of the husbandman," and gained a victory, of which it has been said that no martial event, from the battle of Marathon to that of Waterloo, exerted a greater influence upon human affairs.

In the south, as has been shown, planters and freeholders sprang to arms whenever their homes were threatened. The unsteadiness of the militia in the early battles was nobly atoned for at King's Mountain, at the Cowpens and at Guilford. The

MARION AND HIS MEN.

"Our fortress is the good greenwood,
Our tent the cypress-tree."

names of Morgan and Marion stand, side by side, with those of Herkimer and Stark. "Colonel Marion," complained Cornwallis, "so wrought upon the minds of the people that there was scarcely an inhabitant between the Pedee and the Santee that was not in arms against us."

Around the name of this dashing Southern leader song and story have thrown all the glamour of romance. There may be more of fiction than of fact in the legends that have come down to us, but even these at least breathe the spirit of the times while Bryant's stirring lines fitly emphasize the daring and the recklessness that made the name of " Marion's Men " a power in all that southern land :

> "Our band is few, but true and tried,
> Our leader frank and bold;
> The British soldier trembles
> When Marion's name is told.
> Our fortress is the good greenwood,
> Our tent the cypress-tree;
> We know the forest round us,
> As seamen know the sea.
> We know its walls of thorny vines,
> Its glades of reedy grass,
> Its safe and silent islands
> Within the dark morass.
>
> Wo to the English soldiery
> That little dread us near!
> On them shall light at midnight
> A strange and sudden fear.
> When, waking to their tents on fire,
> They grasp their arms in vain,
> And they who stand to face us
> Are beat to earth again;
> And they who fly in terror, deem
> A mighty host behind,
> And hear the tramp of thousands
> Upon the hollow wind.

"Grave men there are by broad Santee,
   Grave men with hoary hairs;
Their hearts are all with Marion,
   For Marion are their prayers.
And lovely ladies greet our band
   With kindliest welcoming,
With smiles like those of summer,
   And tears like those of spring.
For them we wear these trusty arms,
   And lay them down no more
Till we have driven the Briton,
   For ever from our shore."

It would indeed be but scant justice to the Soldiers of Liberty to omit the praise that is surely due to all such irregular bodies of fighting men as were those who followed Marion and leaders like him. Even to such lawless guerrillas as were the much-maligned "Skinners" who ranged the shores of the Hudson, perpetually harassing the British outposts and forever at deadly feud with their Tory rivals, the "Cowboys," should be accorded a certain meed of praise. From among these came the shrewd and watchful three who, disdaining the bribe of André, frustrated the treason of Arnold and without hope of reward "beyond virtue and an honest sense of duty" saved the patriot cause from the blackest kind of ruin.

It was the Kentucky frontiersmen led on by George Rogers Clarke and John Sevier who turned the tide at the famous battle of King's Mountain, in South Carolina, and changed the whole course of the war in the southern department.

But, while unstinted praise may be accorded to restless militia-man and irregular fighter, it is to the so-called "regular army of the United States" in the days of revolution — known as the Continentals — that glory and honor most heartily belong.

Never rising much above forty thousand men, falling, in the last years of the war, to less than twenty thousand, this army of the Congress was organized, equipped and kept in the field by the tireless energy of Washington and his supporters in the councils of the new-born nation. It was upon them chiefly that their commander depended for discipline, efficiency, obedience and action. In their uniform of buff and blue they were a goodly-appearing and sturdy set of fighters, trim when their coats were new, picturesque even in their rags.

These were the men who stood ever in the gap. Though suffering often for the very necessities of the hard life of the camp, they marched even while they grumbled and fought their bravest even in their direst distress. Believing always in their great commander, spite of faction in Congress and of cabal among their officers, they followed him from defeat to defeat and from victory to victory as loyal through all the hardships of Valley Forge as in the feverish excitement of Monmouth and the final triumph at Yorktown.

Their constancy, their valor and their devotion to the cause of liberty made victory possible. It was because Washington could depend upon this small but solid nucleus of a regular army to carry out his often involved plans for stratagem and action that he was able to wage to its final triumph the slow but successful war that ended in liberty. It was the stubborn determination of these same Continentals that, at the last, flung into utter failure the attempt of the British ministry to enslave three millions of freemen across the western seas.

There is as much truth as poetry, as much force as fire in those well-known lines of McMaster which show us the serried ranks of our first regular army, standing at bay, battling for the freedom of a people:

SOLDIERS OF LIBERTY.

"In their ragged regimentals
Stood the old Continentals,
  Yielding not,
When the Grenadiers were lunging,
And like hail fell the plunging
  Cannon-shot;
  When the files
  Of the isles,
From the smoky night encampment, bore the banner of the rampant
  Unicorn,
And grummer, grummer, grummer rolled the roll of the drummer,
  Through the morn!

"Then with eyes to the front all,
And with guns horizontal,
  Stood our sires;
And the balls whistled deadly,
And in streams flashing redly
  Blazed the fires;
  As the roar
  On the shore,
Swept the strong battle-breakers o'er the green-sodded acres
  Of the plain;
And louder, louder, louder, cracked the black gunpowder,
  Cracking amain!

"Now like smiths at their forges
Worked the red St. George's
  Cannoniers;
And 'the villainous saltpetre'
Rang a fierce, discordant metre
  Round their ears.
  As the swift
  Storm-drift,
With hot sweeping anger, came the horse-guards' clango·
  On our flanks.
Then higher, higher, higher, burned the old-fashioned fire
  Through the ranks!

"Then the old-fashioned Colonel
Galloped through the white infernal
  Powder-cloud;

> And his broad-sword was swinging,
> And his brazen throat was ringing
> Trumpet loud,
> Then the lean
> Bullets flew,
> And the trooper jackets redden at the touch of the leaden
> Rifle-breath,
> And rounder, rounder, rounder, roared the iron six-pounder
> Hurling death!"

It is one of the unfortunate phases of sudden emancipation that certain self-seeking elements among the emancipated assert themselves all too vigorously and strive for position and for power. The arrogance of a brief authority made far too many of those who aspired to be directors or leaders selfish rather than statesman-like, place-hunters rather than patriots.

It is well and wise that in the story of a nation only the good survives. It is better for us and for the memories of our forefathers that in our annals the matchless Declaration of Independence pushes far out of sight the mean-spirited "Conway Cabal," that Bunker Hill and Saratoga and King's Mountain leave but scant place for the factions and the feuds, the spites and the frauds that so often dulled the fires of patriotism and tarnished the glory of our early American Soldiers.

Who to-day ever thinks of the possibility of "an old Continental" being a deserter? And yet there were renegades both before and after the days of Demont the Adjutant; there were traitors fully as criminal as Arnold the General. Who in the victorious America of to-day can believe that in those times that tried men's souls there were, among those high in authority in the American Army, men who undervalued and assailed the measures, the character, even the loyalty of Washington? And yet these hostile elements seemed at some times to be almost in the majority. Not even the military ability of Charles Lee, that arrogant soldier of fortune whom men early in the Revolution styled "the Palladium of America" could save him from an all-consuming jealousy of the commander-in-

WASHINGTON REVIEWING THE CONTINENTAL ARMY.

chief and make him other than a morose comrade, a lagging aid, a half-hearted traitor. Nor could the high rank and commanding station of that favorite of the Congress, General Gates, temper in any degree the vanity, the ambition and the venomous rivalries of the man who displaced Schuyler and listened to belittlements of Washington. To one who studies the unlovely characters of these and such as these even that arch-traitor

Benedict Arnold seems at times their superior. And indeed Arnold's great act of treachery should not blind us to the brilliant qualities of this brave and dashing American soldier. To him may be given much of the credit of the first attack on Ticonderoga, of the movement against Canada, of the night dash on Trenton and of the spirited engagement at Freeman's Farms that made possible the victory at Saratoga. Arrogant and impetuous though he was, angered because other and less-deserving officers had been placed above him in rank, harassed by debt, lightly regarded by Congress, importuned alike by tories and by Englishmen, we must remember that Benedict Arnold even up to the hour of his treachery possessed the confidence and regard of so shrewd a student of men as George Washington himself. In the very defects of his nature lay the pity of his great crime. He was utterly lacking in the patriotism that can calmly brook negligence, in the virtue that can proudly endure injustice.

With examples like these among their superiors and associates it is to the everlasting honor of men like Schuyler and Knox and Green, of Sterling and Wayne, of Lafayette and "Light-Horse Harry" Lee that with the help of that *esprit de corps* that lived in the ragged ranks of the men of Valley Forge they could loyally override so hateful and hostile a spirit as manifested itself in such contemptible conspiracies as "the Conway Cabal" and others of that ilk.

And so to-day it is the valiant and true-hearted officers of the Revolution that we gladly recall. A noble and a gallant list! Warren, unflinching patriot and valiant soldier, who fought and fell a volunteer at Bunker Hill; Knox the Boston bookseller and dear friend of Washington, brave as a lion, "or any braver thing;" Parsons the Connecticut lawyer, an adept in tactics, intrepid on the field; Sterling the impetuous soldier, quick-witted, far-seeing and born for command; Wooster the New York man of wealth and ease who spurned the offer of a command in the British army and used his own fortune to equip and pay his officers and men; Greene, "with the possible exception of Washington," so says Mr. Channing, "the best officer of high rank in the American army;" Schuyler, painstaking, unselfish and ever-valorous, standing, says Daniel Webster, scarcely below Washington in the services he rendered his country; Lincoln, stubborn and unyielding even to the verge of obstinacy, but full of the patriotic fervor that no disaster could dampen; Putnam, brave and valorous in the field though ignorant of the science of war; Henry Lee of Virginia — "Light-Horse Harry" — the Phil Sheridan of the Revolution; Anthony Wayne, the impetuous, magnetic Pennsylvanian, called, at first, " Dandy Wayne " from his extreme punctiliousness as to dress, but in time " Mad Anthony," because of his dash, his recklessness and his daring; Morgan the brilliant backwoodsman and George Rogers Clarke the brave young Western borderer whose gallantry and skill saved the vast western frontier to the United States.

And how this list could be extended! From general and staff officer down through all the grades of rank to the aspiring lieutenant and the still humbler private the names of those brave men who heroically faced defeat, distress and death and made the final triumph possible find, all, their proper place on the imperishable roll of patriotism. From Sergeant Jasper, climbing the riddled staff on Fort Moultrie and nailing at its peak his country's flag amid the whistling storm of British bullets, to plucky Jack Van Arsdale "shinning up" the crippled flag-staff on the battery at New York that the banner of the triumphant Colonies might float in triumph above the heads of the retreating British, the annals of the American Revolution are replete with heroism. It was Sergeant Ezra Lee of Connecticut who, moving stealthily among the war-ships of England, tried with his clumsy infernal machine to blow up the British fleet. It was William Barton the young Providence captain who boldly pushed into the enemy's lines and actually kidnaped the invading commander, the British General Prescott. It was the boatmen of Arnold the traitor who having, all unsuspecting, rowed him to the Vulture man-of-war stoutly refused his bribes and threats to induce them to desert. It was the mutinous soldiers of the Pennsylvania regiments who, when on the march to Princeton to force from Congress redress for unendurable negligence, angrily spurned the offers of Sir Henry Clinton to buy them to his side and hung his messengers as spies. It was the garrison of two that held the fort at Vincennes against eight hundred British troops and after the surrender marched proudly out with all the honors of war.

It would be but partial justice to American blood to fail to remember that in the seven years' contest for freedom there was another side. There were Americans who fought for freedom; there were Americans who remained loyal to their acknowledged king. It was these latter — Royalist, Loyalist, or Tory, call them what we will — who through impulse, interest or a mistaken sense of loyalty remained faithful to the crown of England. During the long contest waged by the revolutionists of America it is claimed that fully thirty thousand provincials entered the British army and fought against their brothers, their neighbors and their former friends. The striking uniform of green in which these battalions of "Loyal Americans" were first clothed gave place before the war was over to the brilliant scarlet that was the badge of British discipline. But all the same whether in green or in scarlet these thirty thousand followers of the banner of the king were American Soldiers.

For fully a century the name of "Tory" has, in America, been the synonym of all that is base in treachery, false in friendship and cruel in war. While the old feuds rankled in the families whose heads had taken different ways in that terrible strife, while personal quarrels intensified political differences this injustice toward those of opposing views was perhaps unavoidable. But the years that leave those hot days of faction further and further in the background should bring to us who look back upon them calmness, candor and dispassionate judgment. If these are to be employed in the study of the past we must accord to the long-despised Tories of the Revolution valor, integrity and renown. They wagered their all on their opinions. They fought and they lost. And we, looking at the result from their stand-point, can surely say with them

> "For Loyalty is still the same
> Whether it win or lose the game."

All over the continent, so we have the assurance of historians and observers, the "loyal" provincial regiments proved on many a stubborn field their worthiness to stand in line with the veterans of the British army. Sir John Johnson, Tory though he was, showed himself yet more merciful than did the "peacock patriots" of Schuyler and the five thousand men of Sullivan, from whose raid on the Six Nations, in 1779, dates, so it is asserted, "the inextinguishable hatred of the red-skins to the United States."

As this struggle between freedom and tyranny was pro-

A GARRISON OF TWO.

"They marched out with all the honors of war."

longed, the armies of that same "tyranny" received constant support from local volunteers. In 1779 New York gave Knyphausen six thousand good troops from among her citizens. The "Gentleman Volunteers" of Boston were commanded by Timothy Ruggles, declared even by his foes to be the best soldier in the colonies. With Clinton in New York in 1782 were over two thousand Loyalists — all battle-scarred veterans. When Cornwallis surrendered at Yorktown he had with him detachments from various regiments of American Loyalists whom continued service and hard fighting had converted into the very best fighting material.

The Pennsylvania Loyalists and the Queen's Rangers of Philadelphia did efficient service for Great Britain. The Loyal Light Horse of Colonel James de Lancey successfully withstood the combined assault of Washington and his French allies. The New York Loyal Volunteers decided by their valor the bloody battle of Eutaw Springs. And these same Tories from Manhattan, after taking part in many a well-fought contest were one of the last regiments in the British service to relinquish their hold on American soil.

The Americans who did not rebel may have been mistaken. Certainly, when the end came, they suffered for their loyalty and lost in exile and poverty the stake they had wagered on their honestly-held opinions. But let us be just. Honor can surely be given where honor is rightly due. Even in such a strife as was this, where brother shot down brother and friend worked vengeance upon friend, we who now look calmly over those frightful battle-grounds can speak, with pride in their valor as soldiers even while we regret the mistake that swayed their judgment and decided their choice, the names of those whom our ancestors condemned as "detested tories" — Drummond of New York, Delancy "the outlaw of the Bronx," Sir John Johnson the feudal lord of the valley of the Mohawk, Ruggles of Massachusetts, De Peyster, the hero of King's Mountain, whose New York "Tories" seven times repelled the furious charge of the "rebels," Thomas and Hovenden and James, whose provincials and refugees were invaluable as light troops while the British lay at Philadelphia — these and many more who might be added prove that even in the tory ranks we have so long been taught to despise there lived the valor, the bravery and the self-sacrifice that have ever been the peculiar pride of the American Soldier.

The smoke of conflict died away when at Yorktown the charge on the British redoubt led by Hamilton and Lafayette showed to Cornwallis the absolute impracticability of longer continuing his defense. The allied troops of America and France — republicanism and absolutism fighting side by side — made the United States a nation.

The seven years of war were ended. A strife that had been of slow but certain growth ever since the days when the first colonists from across the sea set foot on the wild shores of the New World had come to its logical conclusion and a nation of freemen was born. On many a stubborn field, in many a bloody fight the sturdy arm and the valiant heart had proved the moral strength that lay behind them. The first endeavors of the real American Soldier had brought from dependence independence and through patriotism freedom. Henceforth the troops of America were to be the Army of the People.

CHAPTER VI.

THE TROOPS OF DISCONTENT.

ON a certain memorable October morning in the year 1781 a British drummer boy climbed to the parapet of an English redoubt at Yorktown. There, vigorously plying his drumsticks, he sounded the parley. Hostilities ceased. Two days afterward, at two o'clock in the afternoon of the nineteenth of October, the British troops marched out of their works, with colors cased and the soldiers of King George laid down their arms in surrender.

Appropriately enough their drums rattled out the quickstep "The World turned Upside Down." The world was indeed turned upside down so far as all the traditions of power were concerned, for, with that surrender at Yorktown, the American Revolution practically came to an end. Tyranny acknowledged itself defeated and a "parcel of rebels" became a nation of freemen.

But, though the war closed with the surrender of Cornwallis, not for two full years did the troops of England finally leave the land they had so confidently come to conquer. On the twenty-fifth of November, 1783, Sir Guy Carleton evacuated the city of New York. As the British rear guard pushed off from the Battery the advance guard of the Americans — a troop of horse, a regiment of infantry and a company of artillery — filed into the deserted fort. Through the streets of the city that for fully seven years had lain in possession of the soldiers of the English king, sounded the joyful roll of the drums. Escorted by Captain Delavan's "West Chester Light Horse," Washington marched into the city with a veteran following of the Continental troops and the last vestige of England's authority in her former colonies disappeared forever.

But before that day of evacuation and possession arrived the army of the United States had practically been disbanded. When it became evident that no further hostility on the part of England was to be feared the greater portion of the Continental troops was dismissed upon long or indefinite furloughs. On the nineteenth of April, 1783, just eight years to a day from the time of the historic conflict at Lexington, a cessation of hostilities was publicly announced to the American army, and on the eighteenth of October in the same year that army was, by proclamation of the Congress, officially disbanded. This final act took effect on the second of November following and when, on the twenty-fifth of the month, the city of New York was evacuated by the British troops only a small body of veteran soldiers under the command of General Knox represented the American army.

Peace brought respite from war, but it by no means brought satisfaction to those by whom it had been secured. The inspiration of victory is haloed all about with exultation and excitement. The after-happenings of victory are sometimes singularly lacking in enthusiasm. Patriotism is broad and self-sacrificing, but even patriotism needs to be kept alive by such homely necessities as bread and butter. The laborer is worthy of his hire; and when long-promised wages were not forthcoming even the Soldiers of Liberty began to grumble.

The Congress of the United States at a cost of one hundred and forty millions of dollars had waged the war of revolu-

PEACE BY NO MEANS BROUGHT SATISFACTION.

tion to a successful termination. But the cost of this war, small as it may appear in these days of vast expenditures, had loaded the States with a burden of debt greater than they seemed willing or able to carry. The Congress, straining every nerve to force out its plans to success and keep its armies in the field, was scarcely able to meet even the bare necessities of war and when Cornwallis laid down his arms at Yorktown the United States of America found themselves largely in arrears to the very men by whose valor their existence had been rendered possible.

The two years that intervened between the surrender at Yorktown and the evacuation of New York were full of discontent and grumbling. Brave men who had sacrificed so much for the cause they had enlisted to defend felt that the people in whose interests they had fought should at least pay to them the wages that were their due. But even justice seemed to halt. There were exasperating delays on the part of Congress, punctuated only by unfulfilled promises; there was discontent on the part of the army interspersed with frequent mutterings that threatened to break into absolute rebellion. And so the months went slowly by.

With doubts, not only as to the ability but as to the gratitude, even, of the American people the army that had made them a people disbanded. Already in this very year of 1783 the growing discontent among the soldiers had threatened to develop into serious action. The half-rebellious Newburg address which voiced this discontent of the veteran fighters had in it, looked at from their standpoint, a certain amount of justice and excuse. But the very circulation of such an address argued a condition approaching to mutiny; and even injustice is no excuse for insubordination. Washington was not the sort of man to tolerate insurrection. He speedily frowned down an attempt which had the approval even of certain of his colleagues and, by his wisdom, his tact and his firmness, prevented a movement on the part of the army which, if carried out, would have made the Soldiers of Liberty but little better than those military dictators of old — the Prætorian Guards of the soldier-made Cæsars of Rome. The Lancaster revolt of the same year which actually did drive Congress in terror from its chambers and well-nigh upset the government itself was another mistaken act on the part of the discontented soldiers.

These mutterings of discontent ran through several years and were only finally settled by the issue of Continental certificates for the payment of the soldiers' claims. These paper promises to pay, however, were not money. Their value was almost fictitious, and many a poor soldier who had fought for the liberty of the land, when pressed for the very necessities of life, was forced to dispose of these Continental certificates at a ruinous sacrifice — sometimes as low as one sixth of their value.

But the war was over and the army was disbanded. In June, 1784, eighty men represented all that remained of the army of the Congress. Of this number twenty-five were detailed for service at Fort Pitt on the Ohio frontier and fifty-five guarded the almost useless munitions of war at West Point. Sturdy old General Lincoln, the Secretary of War, found himself with no army to direct and retired to private life.

And yet it was evident that soldiers were a necessity. The undefended frontier on the north and west demanded attention. Congress, however, had no power to maintain a standing army in time of peace and when a motion was made to create such an army, even though limited to a few hundred men, so loud was the cry against it by those who deemed it a menace to the liberties of the people that, as a compromise, the several States were invited by Congress to raise their own armies for their own defense. Action was taken on this suggestion, and on the third of June, 1784, an ordinance was passed recommending to the States of Connecticut, New York, New Jersey and Pennsylvania that they raise between them a force of seven hundred men to garrison their frontiers for one year.

When, finally, the Constitution of the United States became the law of the land there existed, in the year 1788, a United States army of the magnificent proportions of five hundred and ninety-five men and two companies of artillery numbering seventy-one non-commissioned officers and privates. These soldiers of the union were distributed among the few military posts kept up by Congress. A small number were stationed at West Point; the remainder were on duty at certain of the stockaded forts in the Western country.

The early years of the new nation were years of disturbance and discontent. People scarcely knew what was to be the character of the government under which they were to live. Until the adoption of the Constitution the several States were leagued together only by a half-way sort of mutual consent that was as brittle and uncertain a bond as would be a rope of sand. Even within the States themselves the law-makers of each commonwealth found themselves at variance with the very people they were elected to represent. Discontent not unfrequently flamed out into real rebellion, mobs and riots were of common occurrence and those who had stood in the ranks of liberty were often all too ready to side with the malcontents and fight against the very authority they had helped to create.

Disturbances growing out of the question of the rightful ownership and occupation of land often developed into actual bloodshed and those who had fought side by side on the battlefields of the Revolution found themselves facing each other, hot and angry, in the strife for possession. One of these interstate disturbances was the attempt by Pennsylvania in 1784 to oust from its hill country about the Wyoming certain families from the East who had settled there under the disputed Connecticut grants. The Commonwealth of Pennsylvania fancying its rights invaded by the coming of these "Yankee" settlers sent detachments from their State army to drive away these old-time "boomers." Coming upon the settlers when floods and fearful weather had well-nigh disheartened them, the Pennsylvania militia, led first by the mean-spirited lawyer Patterson and next by the stern old soldier Armstrong, harried the settlers with fire and with sword and dealt with them as ruthlessly and almost as brutally as had the Tories of Butler and the Indians of Brant in that historic foray that has made the massacre of Wyoming one of the saddest pictures in the Revolutionary story. But brutality found its Nemesis. Among the settlers were men who knew what it meant to fight; and fight they did. At last even the laws of the State stepped in to put a stop to the brutality of Patterson and the treachery of Armstrong, and when these two leaders attempted to resist the authority of the State, they fell before the righteous though eleventh-hour indignation of an awakened people.

It was in the line of similar protests against authority and law that the "military operations" of the troops of discontent were conducted during the years that succeeded the close of the Revolution. Uncertain as to their corporate standing, slowly feeling their way toward a solid footing among the nations of the earth, the people of the newly-united States made many mistakes of judgment, many lapses into faction.

Quick to criticise and all too ready to coin their objections into threats those among the masses who felt themselves unjustly treated by the acts of their own law-makers — "the servants of the people" — were quickly roused to rebel against the constituted authority and to dictate where they should submit. It took long years of harsh experience for the people of the United States to yield unquestionably to the will of the majority.

Out of such unsettled conditions and from such popular protests came much trouble and no little use for the fast-rusting muskets of the Revolution. One of the earliest, as one of the most serious of these disturbances was that known as Shays' Rebellion.

This celebrated rising grew out of questions as to the proprietorship of land, out of the pressure of the hard times, the unwise exactions of those who held claims for money due, the weaknesses of certain laws enacted and especially the attempt, in Massachusetts, to levy State and federal taxes.

In the "ranks of the poor" were many who had been soldiers in the Continental Army. The revolt drew to its support numbers of people in Western Massachusetts, in New Hampshire, Vermont, and even in Eastern New York. The leader was Captain Daniel Shays. He was a man who had seen service in the Revolution and the malcontents who put themselves under his command were speedily drilled into some semblance of military discipline. But an armed mob is much like a pirate crew. Both are outlaws and all attempts at discipline or authority are rated only at second-hand. Leadership is an uncertain quantity. Number One is always the main consideration. So, when the army of Massachusetts, forty-four hundred strong and marshaled by stout old General Lincoln, put itself in motion and actually faced the malcontents in fight the mutinous spirit speedily yielded to the organized forces of Law. There was much threatening and bluster, no little show of resistance, and some fighting, even; but the determination of Lincoln and his militia carried the day and saved not alone the State of Massachusetts but the entire confederation of States from what might have been a disastrous and suicidal popular sentiment.

It is in dealing with the troops of discontent that real discipline best exhibits itself. To be stern and unyielding when occasion demands, to be lenient and forgiving when superiority is once established — this is the only course that wins in all encounters with mobs.

When Shays at the head of two thousand men marched upon the arsenal at Springfield the commandant, General

"NO FEES, NO EXECUTIONS, NO SHERIFF!"

Shepard, thinking to frighten the invaders ordered his men to fire in the air. But the rebel ranks contained too many old soldiers who had smelled powder on real battle-fields and Shepard only recovered from his mistake by an actual and disastrous volley. When General Cobb, an old Revolutionary officer, was menaced by the rioters at Taunton where he was holding court as judge he faced them without an instant's delay and bade them disperse. "Sirs," he said, "you cannot frighten me. I shall either sit here as a judge or die here as a general." "I do not care a rap for your bayonets," shouted that sturdy Revolutionary veteran, Artemas Ward, a judge of Massachusetts but an old soldier as well, when the guards of the rioters barred his way into the court-house at Worcester; "run 'em through me if you dare! I am here to do my duty and I'll do it if I die for it." Firmness in emergencies is almost certain to win and firmness was a quality eminently possessed by the old soldiers of the Revolution.

"No fees, no executions, no sheriff!" was the demand of the rioters at a later day around this same court-house at Worcester. The sheriff, plucky Colonel Greenleaf, looked undismayed upon the triple line of bayonets levelled to bar his progress. "All right," he replied calmly; "if you think the fees for executions are too high — why, I'll hang you all for nothing and high enough to suit you too." "'Burgoyne' Lincoln and his army," was the cry of the rebels in Western Massachusetts when they heard of the military advance against them. But Lincoln and his army were not to be "Burgoyned." The rising of the people to oppose the march of the invading British General whose defeat at Saratoga gave victory to Revolution was not to be repeated when the invaders and the people were of the same kin. Lincoln's spirited march through winter snows showed that this old campaigner, this valiant secretary of war in the Revolutionary days was not to be trifled with and rebellion finally yielded to law. Defeated and dispirited the Troops of Discontent lay down their arms at the feet of Authority, the rebellion broke into pieces and the danger that was so widely feared was at last averted.

This anti-tax rebellion in the North found its counterpart in an anti-tax uprising in the South. The protest of the people of Pennsylvania and Maryland, in 1794, against the federal tax upon spirit distilled within the United States again awoke the troops of discontent who provoked that dramatic episode in American history known as the "Whiskey Insurrection." Seven thousand men marshaled by Bradford the "commander-in-chief" of the revolt pledged themselves to resist to the last the collection of the objectionable tax and speedily laid the whole region within the shadow of the Alleghanies under the terror of mob rule and military despotism. "The whole western country," says Mr. McMaster, "began in the language of that time, to bristle with anarchy-poles. From some floated red flags bearing the name of the rebellious counties. On others were the words 'Liberty or Death,' or 'Liberty and Equality,' or 'No Excise.'"

But the government acted quickly. President Washington made a requisition on the governors of Maryland, Virginia, Pennsylvania and New Jersey, and fifteen thousand men under the command of "Light Horse Harry" Lee — a fighter of the old wars — marched against the malcontents. The battle-cry of the rebels was "Liberty and no Excise." But Liberty to them meant License. "No Excise" meant the free distillation of whiskey. As the troops advanced, the discontented elements fled before Light Horse Harry's men. They could make no stand against organized opposition.

The rising was speedily quelled. It was a bloodless rebellion indeed and though of sufficient force to seem at one time to threaten the very existence of the Union the strength of the military force gathered for its overthrow was so irresistible that danger was averted and once again the Troops of Discontent dispersed at the advance of Authority.

In one way or another, though less serious than were the disturbances already cited, did the chafing of the people of the new nation under unfamiliar and untried laws display itself in resistance and revolt. It is unpleasant to note that the conduct of the soldiers enlisted to quell these insurrections seems to have been open to criticism. Military power, when unchecked, frequently becomes tyranny. The brutalities of Armstrong's troops in the Wyoming trouble of 1784 appear to have found its counterpart in the outrages by the militia of the same Quaker State of Pennsylvania during the short-lived troubles of 1799, known as Fries' Rebellion. These instances of over-zeal, however, were to be expected in so crude and unorganized a body of troops as was the citizen soldiery of the United States in the last days of the eighteenth century.

But this crudeness, so prone to display itself in offensive measures upon unresisting women and children, was compelled to stand a test of quite another sort when brought into battle against the red warriors of the frontier.

The Indians of the west resisted with reasonable justice the encroachments of the settlers who were crowding into their lands beyond the Ohio. Remonstrance and appeal meeting with no attention or resulting only in a contemptuous continuance of occupation, the red-men resorted to their final arguments —the torch, the rifle and the tomahawk. "No white man shall plant corn in Ohio." This was the Indian fiat. "That the threat was not an empty one," says Mr. Black, "soon became apparent. The planter fell in his tracks. The crops were burned and mangled by unseen hands. Death lurked on the Kentucky frontier. There must be war."

The settlers demanded protection. The government responded to their appeal, and in September, 1790, General Josiah

Harmar with an army of fourteen hundred and fifty men was sent into the Ohio country to "discipline" the Indians. But, alas, the boot was found to be quite upon the other foot!

"Never before," says Mr. McMaster, "had such a collection of men been dignified with the name of army." The troops were without discipline, intelligence or decent equipment. The officers were jealous, incompetent and ignorant of military rules. As was to be expected, this collection of "ragged regiments" proved no match for the wary and warlike Indians. The expedition ended, as might have been conjectured, in defeat and disgrace, and the remnant of his army, says Mr. Black, "which Harmar led back to Cincinnati had the unsubdued savages almost continually at their heels."

ON THE FRONTIER.

A second expedition authorized by the President was sent against the Ohio Indians in the autumn of the next year. It mustered two thousand three hundred regulars and six hundred militia and was under the command of General Arthur St. Clair the governor of the Northwest Territory and a prominent officer of the Revolution. This second army met with an even more disastrous defeat than did the troops of Harmar.

Torn with official jealousies, weak in discipline and detail, shamefully supplied with useless equipments by unfaithful government agents, shaking with chills and fever, hungry, tired, sick, and altogether heedless as to their surroundings, St. Clair's army was on the third of November, 1791, surrounded, ambushed and attacked by a host of Indians led on by Brant the half-breed "hero of Wyoming" and utterly and terribly defeated.

Twice outgeneraled and twice so utterly routed! It was a bad record for the American soldier — a fighter who had proved his valor on many a bloody field. But American pluck, without a final struggle, would not leave the Western country to the victorious Indians.

A fresh force was at once enlisted. Five thousand men made up this new army of the West. During the winter of 1791-92 these fresh troops were, according to the direction of President Washington, "trained and disciplined" for the especial service they had entered upon. "Do not spare powder and lead," wrote Washington, "so the men be made marksmen."

The result was an army altogether different from those of Harmar and St. Clair. This army of invasion was rather pompously styled the Legion of the United States. It was especially trained to meet the exigencies of Indian warfare and was divided not into brigades and regiments but into four sub-legions provided with legionary and sub-legionary officers.

The command was given to one of the most popular of the Revolutionary heroes, General Anthony Wayne, the conqueror of Stony Point. "A better officer," says McMaster, "could not have been found." A born soldier, one whose boyhood had been passed in constructing mud-forts and teaching his comrades how to storm redoubts, this gallant Pennsylvanian had fought with valor through the Revolution, had been decorated by Congress for his bravery and enthusiastically nicknamed by his soldiers and the people "Mad Anthony Wayne."

He assumed the command determined to win. And he

THE BATTLE OF TIPPECANOE.

did win. With an army made efficient through careful drill, through discipline, appropriate equipment and all the requisites that its unfortunate predecessors had lacked the "Legion of the United States" marched into the Ohio country, made a vigorous attack upon the Indians and their Canadian allies and in the bloody battle of the Maumee fought on the twentieth of August, 1794, with all the valor of Monmouth and all the dash of Stony Point, utterly routed and scattered the Indian foeman. "Such was the impetuosity of the charge, by the first line of infantry," so runs General Wayne's report, "that the Indian and Canadian militia and volunteers were driven from their coverts in so short a time that but a part of the legion could get up in season to participate in the action."

Almost as ferocious and still more famous because it made the record of a brave American soldier and a popular American president was the battle of Tippecanoe. This celebrated Indian engagement was fought within the limits of the Illinois country in the year 1811. Uniting for the annihilation of the white man, under their politic and patriotic chieftain Tecumthe, the Indians of the northwest confederated for white destruction, burst upon the little army of General Harrison in the dark of the early morning of the seventh of November, 1811. It was an unwise move for the red-man and was brought about, not by the genius of Tecumthe, but by the influence of his uncanny-looking kinsman "The Prophet." Harrison's nine hundred men sturdily stood their ground. The battle was long and bloody, the loss in officers was especially noticeable, but the Indians were defeated and Tecumthe's carefully-laid plan for an Indian confederacy was forever overthrown.

In all the hostile encounters succeeding the Revolution

there was, indeed, much that must astonish and annoy the patriotic student of American character who cannot precisely square the cowardice and unruliness, the crudeness and the lack of discipline with the standing of Revolutionary veterans and the traditions of American valor. But, even while admitting the existence of these negative qualities, there must be found in the story of those immature days much that can brighten an uninteresting record and illumine an often-clouded picture.

There was, as we have seen, alike pluck and courage in the days of discontent. And, even in Harmar's undisciplined foray, the skill and daring of such true-hearted soldiers as Major Fontaine of the Regulars shed a certain glory over the gloom of defeat. The spirited bayonet charge of Colonel Darke, roused to fury at the fall of his son, almost retrieved the disasters of St. Clair. The pluck and valor of Anthony Wayne's nine hundred, who at the Maumee Rapids routed a British and Indian force of more than twice their number, were emphatically displayed in deeds of personal prowess that were inspired by the bravery and bearing of the intrepid commander.

"In what light, sir," demanded the British commandant, Major Campbell, "am I to view such near approaches of an American army almost within reach of the guns of a post belonging to His Majesty the King of Great Britain?"

"The muzzles of my small arms, sir, in yesterday's fight gave the most full and most satisfactory answer to your question," Wayne defiantly replied. "Had the action continued until the Indians were driven to the protection of the post you mention even the guns of that post would not have impeded the progress of the victorious army under my command."

On the field of Tippecanoe — that bloody battle in the dark

— the vigilance and valor of General Harrison brought to his name a lasting renown and inspired the men who won that historic victory; for Tippecanoe, though a triumph dearly bought, was far-reaching in its results.

"Where is the captain of this company?" the general demanded as, peering through the gloom he saw on the high ground where the prairies meet a little body of men gallantly holding their own. "Dead, sir," said the young Ensign Tipton. "Where are the lieutenants?" "Dead." "Where is the ensign?" "I am here." "Stand fast, my brave fellow," said the general with a look of approval at the gallant little band and its no less gallant leader; "one moment longer and I will relieve you." The relief came and the victory of Tippecanoe was assured.

ANTHONY WAYNE.

For any lack of valor, of discipline or of martial moods in the days of conflict that make up the story of the Troops of Discontent and the Soldiers of Immaturity we must look for the cause to the very composition and methods of the Americans themselves.

The Revolution was over. A land, wasted by seven years of war, demanded immediate attention or the work of years of preparation would be lost. Beyond the battle-scarred land lay the wildernesses of the vaster West. They were full of promise, fertile of hope, and called for men to conquer, to settle and to develop them.

To all such home-builders further strife was repugnant. The political sky, too, was so clouded, so full of warring elements, so dark with uncertainties that, to the majority of the people, the army was an unpleasant and unprofitable national incubus, the life of the soldier was deemed as but the last resort of the shiftless, the drone or the outcast.

And yet, notwithstanding the popular objections to a standing army, Congress managed to have under its control, even from the very adoption of the Constitution, at least the shadow of such an army.

The War Department of the United States was organized on the seventh of August, 1789, with General Knox as the first Secretary of War. He found a standing force of six hundred and seventy-two available men as the "bulwark" of the new nation—a weak enough bulwark for so undefended a land! From the date of the organization of the Department to the War of 1812 the Secretaries of War were, respectively: Henry Knox, Timothy Pickering, James McHenry, Samuel Dexter, Roger Griswold, Henry Dearborn and William Eustis. Of these, all except Dexter were veterans of the Revolution, but the incoherencies, the frail finances and, above all, the national animosity to a standing army gave our first Secretaries little in the way of material and much in the way of worry.

As Indian wars and international disputes warranted an increasing force the troops of the United States grew from the paltry seven hundred of 1789 to somewhat more respectable proportions. In 1792 this force was increased to 5120 men, in 1794 it fell to 3629; it rose to 5144 in 1804, dropped to 3278 in 1807, and, in 1810, footed up 7154. Between these years, too, its generals-in-chief were of an equally shifting character. Washington was succeeded by Knox in 1783, Knox by Harmar in 1788, Harmar by St. Clair in 1791, St. Clair by Wayne in 1792, Wayne by Wilkinson in 1796, Wilkinson by Washington in 1798 and Washington again by Wilkinson in 1800.

Washington's term as Lieutenant-General began on the third of July, 1798, just twenty-two years to a day after his assuming command of the Revolutionary troops on the commons of Cambridge. It was his last service to the American people and was the result of the popular war-wave that swept the land when, in 1798, the insults of France, steeped in the fanatical fury of a righteous revolution unrighteously upheld, almost drove the former allies into war.

Throughout the States the black cockade was the symbol of patriotism; the old fervor of the fighting days returned and the doggerel of the time, sung and whistled in every town, gave the key note of determination:

> "Americans then fly to arms,
> And learn the way to use 'em;
> If each man fight to 'fend his rights
> The French can't long abuse 'em."

The war fever grew. Line-of-battle ships sprang from hastily-laid stocks. Along the Atlantic coast forts were traced out, built or strengthened. Volunteers rushed to the militia recruiting offices and, as the citizen soldiers of America pledged themselves anew to the defense of the land they loved, they shouted huzza! and yet again huzza! to the most popular of all the toasts and sentiments of the day: "Millions for defense but not one cent for tribute!"

But neither defense nor tribute became necessary. Napoleon the Shrewd as well as the Great, recognized the unwisdom of making another foe in the "nation of debaters" across the western sea. France recalled her hasty words and stopped her hostile ways. The allies of old became friends once more and the army of the United States was reduced to a peace footing. The militia regiments dwindled away; muster days lost their dramatic expectancies and not until 1812, when the old antagonist, Britain, sought to force brutality into battle and contempt into conflict was there need or call for the active services of the American Soldier.

And as the century died there died with it the great soldier who had by his wisdom, his strategy and his indomitable will led the way along which the thirteen colonies marched into freedom. In 1799 Washington died — the leading historic figure of the eighteenth century, the soldier who first in war was also the statesman first in peace and has ever since been the ideal patriot, first in the hearts of his countrymen.

CHAPTER VII.

A LEADERLESS WAR.

THERE stood, in the year 1812, in that far Northwest where the waters of three great inland seas unite for their onward course to the distant ocean, a solitary outpost garrisoned by the soldiers of the United States — the fort on Mackinaw. A small but important post, the country that it defended had been for generations the scene of contest. Here French and Indians, here English and French, here Americans and Englishmen had warred for the possession of the western water-ways into Lakes Michigan and Superior. Finally delivered up by the British in 1795 it was, in this month of July, 1812, held by a little garrison of fifty-seven American soldiers under command of Lieutenant Hanks.

Remote from civilization, surrounded only by the waters and forests of the vast Northwest, this slender band of defenders heard but little from the world without and still less from their official superiors — the dilatory War Department at Washington. Forty miles to the northeast, upon St. Joseph's Island in the

Sault St. Marie, stood the nearest English post, garrisoned by a small detachment of British regulars under command of Captain Roberts.

On the morning of the seventeenth of July, 1812, Lieutenant Hanks, looking out from his quarters, was surprised to see no signs of life in the little fur-trading settlement that had sprung up below the American post. Sending out to ascertain the cause he was astounded to learn that, during the preceding night, a force of more than a thousand men — British, Canadians and Indians — had been led from the British fort above against the American post. But still more astounded was he when he learned that war had actually been declared between Great Britain and the United States, and that a British officer waited below, flag in hand, as a messenger from Captain Roberts, demanding the surrender of Fort Mackinaw.

Resistance was impossible. Dazed, overawed and entirely unprepared for defense Lieutenant Hanks had no alternative but to surrender. With a negligence that was as stupid as it was unpardonable the War Department at Washington delayed sending to the posts on the Western frontier any notification of the declaration of war. The British authorities had been quick to act. And thus it came to pass that an important military post among the great lakes fell without a blow to the alert and better-informed soldiers of England.

This disaster at Mackinaw was but an index to the conduct of what is known in the history of America as the War of 1812. Negligence, delay, " a miserly economy " and an utter lack of trained troops impeded the American operations from the very outset. Forts were surrendered, important posts abandoned, battles lost and plans of invasion disastrously brought to naught by the utter lack of competent leaders and the timid and wavering ways of those in authority at Washington. "History," says Mr. Roosevelt, " has not yet done justice to the ludicrous and painful folly and stupidity of which the government founded by Jefferson and carried on by Madison was guilty, both in its preparation for and in its way of carrying on this war; nor is it yet realized that the men just mentioned and their associates are primarily responsible for the loss we suffered in it and the bitter humiliation some of its incidents caused us."

It has for years been with too many Americans the fashion to speak of the War of 1812 as a successful resistance of the arms of England by the army and navy of the United States. Of the navy this may have been true; but so far as the army was concerned its part in the second war with England was very far from being a glorious round of successes. This, a study of the records will only too plainly show. The land operations of the War of 1812 are, as one writer has declared, " neither cheerful reading for an American nor interesting to a military student." Almost the only bright spot in the long catalogue of disaster was the dramatic battle of New Orleans, won by a general who, up to that time, had scarcely been esteemed a leader and fought after peace had been declared — a needless battle and a useless victory.

Self-inspection is one of the best remedies for a tendency to boasting and vainglory. Let us hastily glance at the facts. Quickly following the fall of Fort Mackinaw came the failure of Hull's campaign on the Michigan frontier, the defeat of Van Horne by Tecumthe and his Indians, the cruel massacre at Fort Dearborn, now Chicago, and the cowardly surrender of Detroit. The invasion of Canada by Van Rensselaer ended with the defeat of the Americans at Queenstown and the astounding refusal of the American militia-men to cross to the succor of their countrymen. The failure of the ridiculous and vaporizing Smythe in a second invasion of Canada was in no degree lightened by the successful defense at Ogdensburg, where one thousand Americans succeeded in driving off four hundred British besiegers; for, early in the next year of the war (1813), Ogdensburg fell.

Winchester's terrible defeat on the river Raisin and the bloody massacre of his troops by the inhuman Proctor was scarcely retrieved by the defense of Fort Meigs and the brave stand of Croghan at Fort Stephenson. Harrison's invasion of Canada did lead to a victory on the Thames where thirty-five hundred Americans routed an inferior force of sixteen hundred British and Indians and ended in the death of the heroic Tecumthe; but the capture of Fort George by the Americans was, soon after, altogether neutralized by the spiritless and unnecessary surrender of the fort to the British. Then came the utter defeat of Chandler's invasion of Canada, the capture of Fort Niagara and the destruction of Buffalo, and the total failure of still another invasion of Canada led on by that military mountebank, the American general Wilkinson — a commander whom the indignant Scott hotly denounced as "an unprincipled imbecile."

The army of Hampton on Lake Champlain seemed scarcely to dare lift a gun in protest while British invaders plundered Plattsburgh and Burlington. The three principal engagements of the year 1813 were little more than routs of incompetent troops led by incapable generals; they were victories for England when they should easily have been, instead, victorious engagements won by superior forces of Americans.

Indeed, the opening years of this War of 1812 were neither honorable to the American soldier nor helpful to the American cause. For twelve years the war had been plainly foreseen. England's tyrannical encroachments upon American commerce, her contemptuous disregard of treaty stipulations and the rights of American seamen, her endeavors to antagonize and inflame the Indians within American territory and her unwarranted

AT WORK ON THE FORTIFICATIONS IN 1812.

trespassing upon the Western frontier had gradually forced America into armed resistance. And yet for this resistance no suitable preparation had been made by the government of the United States.

It is true that a slight increase had been made in the number and strength of the regular army. By an act of Congress in 1808 five regiments of infantry, one of riflemen and one each of light artillery and light dragoons had been added to the army. This increased the force, by the year 1810, to nearly eight thousand men.

But popular approval did not go out kindly to such a strengthening of the army; even its slow development therefore was almost in spite of the protest of the majority. With the growth of the war-fever, however, bombast developed into action. When the news of war came to the ears of the people men of all classes awoke to their need for action and hastened to offer their services or to bear a helping hand in rearing defenses and strengthening fortifications.

This sudden haste toward national defense however could not make up for the lack of material and the supineness of government. President Madison, contrary to his own desires, was forced into war; but the politicians who had brought about the conflict had been so lax in military preparations that, as Professor Soley says, " while securing a political victory they prepared the way for a series of military defeats."

How discouraging were these defeats during the opening years of the war we have already seen. And indeed it does seem almost incredible that a strong and vigorous people, angered over the invasion of their rights upon the seas and battling for the possession of those Western frontiers which they desired to secure as their children's inheritance, should lack either the warlike spirit or the warrior's valor. It is for us to remember, however, that it was not so much the lack of these fighting qualities as the absolute dearth of leaders that made the land operations of the American Soldier during the War of 1812 so sorry a page in American history.

The fighting strength of the nation just previous to the declaration of war was estimated in the militia returns of the States as very close upon seven hundred thousand men. Estimates however are not always a safe foundation. Numbers are often as shrinking as are the volunteers themselves when the bugles sound for action. The main dependence of a nation in the early stages of any war must rest rather upon well-furnished officers than upon the long muster-rolls of its recruits. And it is now generally conceded that the Army of the United States entered upon the second war with England "with few officers of professional training or traditions." The generals to whom commands were at first assigned were but superanuated soldiers who had outlived the fire, as they had the days, of the distant Revolution. The militia too were crude and unmanageable, with more taste for discussing the questionable plans of their superiors than for following them.

And so, with raw levies unable to learn with sufficient speed the demands of military life and discipline, with incompetent generals who had either outgrown their fighting days or had not enough military intelligence to drill or to direct their followers, with distracted counsels among the rulers of the nation and with but a grudging support from the very people who talked the loudest about rights and privileges the United States of America essayed to cross swords with one of the most warlike of European nations. It was a power whose soldiers had faced the victorious armies of the great Napoleon, whose grenadiers were led on by generals schooled to the ways of war in the wild Mahratta battles of India or in the more momentous conflicts that had checked the career of the greatest of modern conquerors in the stubborn battles of the Spanish peninsula.

1813 was a year of failure for the American arms. 1814

was but little better. The exigencies of a losing fight were, however, developing certain capable commanders in the ranks of American captains. These generals indeed did not rise to the position of real leaders, but their very impatience over the disgrace that was clouding the name of the American Soldier gave them so much determination that their earnest examples and their tireless efforts began at last to infuse something like discipline and effectiveness into the wavering ranks of an undisciplined army.

In the swamps and morasses of the distant South the sturdy and unyielding Jackson was learning in the savage school of Indian warfare that untiring vigilance and sleepless energy that were to work such terrible results upon the veteran troops of England in the opening days of 1815. The victory of Tohopeka, by which on the twenty-seventh of January, 1814, General Andrew Jackson, after a furious fight of more than five hours, broke forever the power of the Creek Confederacy, found its still greater results in the more glorious but utterly needless victory at New Orleans. In the north, upon the Canadian frontier, the patience and persistence of Winfield Scott imparted a steadiness and efficiency to those uncertain volunteers who had rallied to the defense of the northern border. The ludicrous failure of Wilkinson with which the campaign of 1814 had opened was fully retrieved by the gallantry of Scott's brigade at Chippeway and the obstinate courage of that same band of fighters at Lundy's Lane. And yet neither Chippeway nor Lundy's Lane can rightfully be claimed as American victories. They were simply not American defeats; and it is the chief glory of both these savage actions that they showed the spirit that really slumbered in American fighting men and by their obstinacy changed British contempt into

British caution. Even William James, most prejudiced of all the English chroniclers of this war with America, is forced to admit that, "upon the whole, the American troops fought bravely; and the conduct of many of the officers would have done honor to any service."

And yet that same year of 1814 saw the glory of American endeavor at Chippeway and Lundy's Lane clouded by the shame of American feebleness on the Chesapeake. No page in American history is more disgraceful than that which tells of the invasion of Maryland by the British troops and how a small force of the red-coated enemy put to flight a largely superior force of Americans at Bladensburg, set the whole American government in hasty and undignified retreat from the American capital, captured Washington, destroyed the public buildings, scattered the Americans by a vigorous bayonet charge at North Point and spread terror and dismay through all the Chesapeake region.

"That Americans," says Professor Soley, "when properly led could make as good fighting material as any other people, had been shown in the Revolution and was still more forcibly shown, later, in the war with Mexico and in the Civil War; but in 1812–15 they were without leaders. With the exception of Brown, Jackson, Scott, Gaines, Harrison, Macomb, and Ripley, most of whom were at first in subordinate positions, there were few general officers worthy of the name and it required only the simplest strategic movement to demonstrate their incompetency." "The British regulars," says Mr. Roosevelt, "trained in many wars thrashed the raw troops opposed to them whenever they had anything like a fair chance. Our defeats were exactly such as any man might have foreseen and there is nothing to be learned by the student of military matters from the follies committed by incompetent commanders and untrained troops when in the presence of skilled officers having under them disciplined soldiers."

It is a truth not to be disguised that this War of 1812, which from the outset was so marred by "the humiliating surrenders, abortive attacks and panic routs" of the land forces of the Union, was turned into victory and success by the daring and the dash of the American Sailor.

But this is the darker side of the annals. It would indeed be a disgraceful stain on the soldier's record of American valor if the story of our second war with England rested here. With a brave people, out of defeat springs new determination; out of humiliation, heroism.

It is this regal purpose that we can read between the lines as we trace that record of disaster by land and of victory on the sea. The story of the land operations which began in loss at Mackinaw and ended in triumph at New Orleans is an ever-increasing assurance of the growing valor, persistence and patriotism of the American Soldier. Hampered by all the restrictions that must spring from a weak and wavering government, from internal dissensions and political strifes, from raw and unsteady comrades and from the disheartening incompetency of generals who would be leaders but could not, the soldiers of the United States learned steadiness from disaster and determination from disgrace, and gradually developed into seasoned fighters who could play on even terms with the British invaders.

Thus, step by step, the militia-man became the veteran. The gallantry of Croghan and his weakened garrison at Fort Stephenson, the irresistible charge of the mounted riflemen of Kentucky who broke the line of Proctor's regulars at the

CAPTAIN HINDMAN AT FORT GEORGE.

battle of the Thames showed, each of them, that even thus early in the war the old-time American valor was by no means a forgotten quantity.

The terrible bayonet charge with which in fair fight the valiant fellows of Scott's brigade hurled backward in flight an equal force of British regulars and turned the day at Chippeway; the inspiring valor with which at Lundy's Lane the modest but gallant Miller led his men against the battery on the hill and carried it by an assault that was as full of danger as it was of bravery; the equal gallantry with which Ripley and his comrades held that same captured hill-top against three desperate assaults by the enemy's entire force; the bold and masterly sortie from beleaguered Fort Erie, by which General Gaines scattered the British besiegers, saved his post and, indeed, the whole New York frontier — a dash which for brilliancy, so one author asserts, " has never been excelled by any event in the same scale in military history' — these, as the war progressed, were convincing proofs that American courage only needed opportunity to display itself even upon the most uncertain field.

When at Lundy's Lane Colonel James Miller was ordered to storm and capture the British battery to which reference has already been made and which, crowning a hill-top, was really the key to the enemy's position he made but the simple reply: " I'll try, sir" — and took it! "If success attend my steps," wrote, in a letter to his father, that General Pike who in 1813 led into Canada the successful invasion that cost him his life, " honor and glory await my name; if defeat still shall it be said that we died like brave men and conferred honor, even in death, on the American name." "We demand the joint use with you of this Lake Ontario as a public highway, or you shall not detach your troops," said Colonel Van Rensselaer, standing under a flag of truce in British headquarters. This audacious demand being denied, the young American colonel declared that all negotiations for an armistice were at an end. The boldness of his stand angered the British officers. They sprang to their feet while General Sheaffe, their commander, significantly placing his hand on his sword-hilt said sternly, "Sir, you take high ground." Nothing daunted by this hostile attitude of his enemies Van Rensselaer as quickly clapped hand to his own sword-hilt and replied " I do, sir, and will maintain it ; but you dare not detach the troops." Such pluck found recognition from the British soldier; he begged Van Rensselaer's pardon for his hastiness and agreed to the joint use of the Lake. On the ninth of May, 1813, there came a lull in the vigorous bombardment of Fort Meigs. Under a flag of truce Major Chambers representing the British besiegers was introduced into the presence of General Harrison, the commander of the American post. He presented a demand for the immediate surrender of the fort. "Assure General Proctor," was Harrison's reply, " that he will never have this post surrendered to him upon any terms. Should it fall into his hands it will be in a manner calculated to do him more honor than any capitulation could possibly do." So pluckily did Harrison keep his word that the " butcher of Frenchtown " fell back baffled and defeated.

The spirit that lived in such words as these that came from the lips of officers, gradually found its counterpart in the subordinates or privates who fought under them. The younger officers quickly imbibed this growing confidence and determination. We read of one passage of arms within sound of the roar of Niagara marked for especial brilliancy and valor in which not a single American officer engaged in the fight was above the rank of captain. It was here that young Captain Wool — destined to become in years after a grizzled veteran in the Mexican War — already sorely wounded but still eager for action, under a killing fire from the enemy charged up the hill at Fort George and won the heights of Lewiston. It was this same brave young fellow of twenty-four who later in the day when a less daring brother officer would have displayed the flag of surrender indignantly snatched the fluttering handkerchief from the bayonet point and cheered on his men to such a desperate bayonet charge that the enemy broke before his impetuosity while the Forty-Ninth Grenadiers, one of the most famous of the British regiments, turned and fled in dismay. The "I'll try, sir!" of Miller at Lundy's Lane was a text upon which thereafter many a dashing officer and many a valiant private preached by his acts a stirring sermon on American valor.

Notwithstanding the lack of example in the higher officers in this leaderless war the records of the privates who fought through it are by no means barren of pluck and heroism. It is said that when Winchester surrendered his command to the British butcher Proctor many of the soldiers declared that they would not submit to the terms. They had come there to fight the British and fight they would. They plead with their officers to stand firm; some even wept tears of disgrace and mortification and declared they would rather die on the field. When ordered finally to lay down their arms in surrender they threw them upon the ground with such rage and indignation as to shiver the stocks from the barrels and they declared to the British soldiers that their general had sold out "the greatest set of game-cocks that ever came from old Kentuck."

At the time of the disastrous British attack on Washington and the surrounding country in 1814 Private John O'Neil was the only faithful militia-man in the "Potato Battery" at Havre de Grace. When all his comrades had fled he sturdily stuck to his guns while fifteen British barges pounded away at the little fort. While the grapeshot flew thickest about him

PACKENHAM'S CHARGE AT THE BATTLE OF NEW ORLEANS.

he coolly loaded, served and fired the nine-pounder mounted on the battery and then, being wounded by the recoil, retreated to a nail factory where he kept up the fight until his powder was exhausted. Wounded and without ammunition then only did he admit himself defeated and surrender himself and his two empty muskets to a British officer.

On the eve of battle near Fort Wayne, General Harrison read to the volunteers under his command some of the regulations and restrictions that were made necessary by the articles of war. He then declared that if any among the volunteers did not feel willing to submit to such restrictions they might return home. Only one man availed himself of this offer. Thereupon several of his acquaintances, receiving permission to escort him out of the camp, mounted him upon a rail, carried him to the river and there ruthlessly ducked him again and again in order as they said "to wash away all his patriotism."

At the battle of Frenchtown Major Graves, gallantly leading his men against an overwhelming force of the enemy, fell with a shot in his knee. Still cheering on his men he cried out, "Boys, I am wounded; never mind me, but fight on."

At the capture of Fort George, Hindman a Maryland captain, belying the suggestion of his name, was almost the first man in the fort. Hearing a rumor that the enemy were to blow up the works rather than let them pass into American hands Hindman at the sword's point, compelled a British sergeant to lead him to the magazine. Careless of personal danger he snatched away the rapidly burning fuse that was fast approaching the powder and thus saved the fort and his comrades.

Instances of personal valor such as these could be multiplied in proof of the assertion that while this leaderless War of 1812 was deficient in the brilliant enterprises and dashing achievements that, more than all else, give to war its romance and its glitter, there still lived in the hearts of the people that individual bravery and dauntless courage without which, when pushed to the wall by its foes, a nation cannot hope for success.

Militia-men might hesitate, waver and run away; regulars might fail when most they should have been relied upon; commanders might blunder, wrangle and even show the white feather, but the valor of one man can often save a host from disgrace; the desperation of a forlorn hope outlives the cowardice of an army.

So through the war, marked as it was with records of American imbecility and British inhumanity, the development of the national courage went slowly forward. Out of unsteadiness grew discipline, out of foolish boastings came stern determination, out of faintheartedness sprang valor. The irresponsible State detachments, amenable to their own officers, jealous of the regulars and of the war-department officers, gradually merged their personalities and their local names of "Fusileers," "Hussars," and "Rifles" into the broader title of American Soldiers and proved, in such fights as Chippeway, their right to the name of warriors and in such engagements as New Orleans their appreciation of what that name really meant.

"We have now got an enemy who fights as bravely as ourselves," wrote an English officer after the battle of Chippeway. "They have now proved to us that they only wanted to acquire a little discipline; they have now proved to us what they are made of; and they are the same sort of men as those who captured whole armies under Burgoyne and Cornwallis; they are neither to be frightened nor to be silenced."

The great battle of the war was unquestionably the action at New Orleans. Had but the ocean cable then spanned the Atlantic, like a living cord uniting the nations, the news of peace flashed beneath the waters would have rendered New Orleans unnecessary. But on the other hand it would have withheld from the crest of the American soldier one of his most proudly-worn trophies; it would have taken from the hereditary taunt of the hater of England its severest sting. Bloody and unnecessary though it was, it stands in history as so notable a monument to the skill of a great commander and the valor of a volunteer army that it finds fitting mention in the story of the American Soldier.

As first looked at this battle of New Orleans seems full of inconsistencies. Ten thousand British regulars, the bravest and most hardy of the veteran fighters of Wellington's Peninsular Army, with a record of six years of uninterrupted success, were to face in fight less than five thousand soldiers drawn from the fighting stock of a nation deficient at that time in all the elements that constitute successful warfare. To be sure the undisciplined five thousand were shielded behind mud-breastworks; but what was that to the valiant warriors who had stormed the fortifications at Toulouse, and Badajos, and Ciudad Rodrigo? With the exception of Wellington no general officer in the British army was counted the equal of Sir Edward Packenham. Opposed to him was a leader unskilled in the science of war, sadly deficient in the knowledge of tactics and utterly lacking in those personal qualifications necessary to what is known as the courtesy of camps. He was in the eyes of the brilliant British general only "a grizzled old bush-fighter whose name had never been heard of outside of his own swamps."

But it is the unexpected that is always happening. If Jackson was lacking in the art of war he was possessed of that higher military genius that rises superior to science and to tactics. His conquest of the warlike Indian tribes of the South had taught him a wariness that could never know surprise, an energy that was tireless, and a courage that was as unfaltering as it was obstinate. With almost no support from the demoralized national government, drawing his soldiery (with the exception of seven hundred regulars) from the widely-scattered settlements of the southern border, he massed his men behind a low line of mud-breastworks, manned his guns with frontier fighters who were sharp of eye and sure of aim and waited for the morning.

It was the eighth of January, 1815. "At last," says Mr. Roosevelt, "the sun rose. As its beams struggled through the morning mist they glinted on the sharp steel bayonets of the English, where their scarlet ranks were drawn up in battle array, but four hundred yards from the American breastworks. There stood the matchless infantry of the island king, in the pride of their strength and the splendor of their martial glory; and as the haze cleared away they moved forward, in stern silence, broken only by the angry, snarling notes of the brazen bugles. At once the American artillery leaped into furious life; and, ready and quick, the more numerous cannon of the invaders responded from their hot, feverish lips. Unshaken amid the tumult of that iron storm the heavy red column moved steadily on toward the left of the American line, where the Tennesseeans were standing in motionless, grim expectancy. Three fourths of the open space was crossed, and the eager soldiers broke into a run. Then a fire of hell smote the British column. From the breastwork in front of them the white smoke curled thick into the air, as, rank after rank, the wild marksmen of the backwoods rose and fired, aiming low and sure. As stubble is withered by flame, so withered the British column under that deadly fire; and, aghast at the slaughter, the reeling files staggered and gave back. Packenham, fit captain for his valorous host, rode to the front, and the troops, rallying round him, sprang forward with ringing cheers. But once again the pealing rifle-blast beat in their faces; and the life of their dauntless leader went out before its scorching and fiery breath.

"With him fell the other general who was with the column, and all of the men who were leading it on; and, as a last resource, Keane brought up his stalwart Highlanders; but in vain the stubborn mountaineers rushed on, only to die as their comrades had died before them, with unconquerable courage, facing the foe, to the last. Keane himself was struck down; and the shattered wrecks of the British column, quailing before certain destruction, turned and sought refuge beyond reach of the leaden death that had overwhelmed their comrades.

ANDREW JACKSON.

"Nor did it fare better with the weaker force that was to assail the right of the American line. This was led by the dashing Colonel Rennie, who, when the confusion caused by the main attack was at its height, rushed forward with impetuous bravery along the river bank. With headlong fury Rennie flung his men at the breastworks and, gallantly leading them, sword in hand, he, and all around him, fell, riddled through and through by the balls of the riflemen. Brave though they were, the British soldiers could not stand against the singing, leaden hail, or if they stood it was but to die. So in rout and wild dismay they fled back along the river bank, to the main army."

"By eight o'clock," says Mr. Thompson, "the harvest was over; the red field of the eighth of January had been mowed. In front of Humphrey's batteries stretched the tangled windrows of mangled dead; prone beneath the deadly riflemen of Beale's little command the red-coats lay in heaps; the swaths cut down by Carrol and Adair were horrible to see. What slaughter; what a victory! Over two thousand British lay dead or helpless on the field. And what of Jackson's little army? How many killed? Just eight men! How many wounded? Thirteen men, and no more!"

It was a victory as complete as it was surprising. But while the creoles of New Orleans fought with a valor all the more desperate because they were defending their homes from pillage, while the rifles of Tennessee and Kentucky spread a havoc that was as certain as it was terrible, while the pirates of Barataria and the sailor-volunteers added alike picturesqueness and ferocity to that dim fighting in a fog it must not be forgotten that the credit of the victory at New Orleans mainly belongs to the man whose foresight planned and whose courage effected the result — Andrew Jackson, the general.

It was a brilliant close to a war that lacked brilliancy. It was a dramatic ending to a conflict that, upon the land at least, had, for the most part, been listless and tame indeed; it was the final vindication, in an era when such a setting right seemed almost impossible, of the pluck and the bravery, the steadfastness and the valor of the American Soldier.

Great generals rise but seldom above the level of their troops. Signal victories, attained by the indomitable will of one leader, are almost exceptions in history. Without the rank and file the commander would be less than a unit. But the battle of New Orleans was one of these exceptions. The genius of its valiant leader rose superior to all obstacles.

The credit for the one victory of the War of 1812 rightly belongs to one man — Andrew Jackson of Tennessee — "who," once more to quote from Mr. Roosevelt's summing-up of the fight, " with his cool head and quick eye, his stout heart and strong hand, stands out in history as the ablest general the United States produced from the outbreak of the Revolution down to the beginning of the great Rebellion." The leaderless war was closed by a leader indeed.

CHAPTER VIII.

WARS AND RUMORS OF WAR.

THE bells of 1815 as they rang out the glad tidings of peace lulled a nation to rest. The war was over. The people were thankful. The good ship Fortune, sailing into New York harbor on the eleventh of February in that year of peace with the news of the treaty of Ghent, bore precious freight. The rancors of divided councils were settled and a distracted land set to work to recover as speedily as possible from the loss of the hundred million hard dollars and the thirty thousand good lives that the war had cost.

The motley militia-men of the several States returned to their homes; at least three thousand of those thirteen thousand stiff parade hats and uncomfortable-looking uniforms that had been the distinguishing mark of the regulars of 1812 were laid aside and the army of the United States was reduced to a peace footing of less than ten thousand men.

But though at peace with the outside world there was still call for musket and bayonet, saber and spur. The feeble power of Spain though ever so feebly defended was a menace to the growth of the republic in the south and west. The constant intrigues of intriguing England kept alive a continual boundary trouble in the north. Upon the fringe of forest that marked the country's vast frontier rested the ever-present dread of Indian attack and ferocity. It behooved the nation to sleep on its arms.

Scarcely had the echoes of the victorious guns at New Orleans died away when trouble broke out in that section of the southern land known as East Florida. British agents stirred the Indians to hostility and the blacks to revolt, working their inhuman schemes in the Spanish territory that touched the American border. Here first, in 1816, Colonel Clinch took the field against the half-breed marauders and with a picked force of United States regulars stormed the combined negro and Indian stronghold which the English had established on the Appalachicola River; but trouble still continued and was only brought to an end by the prompt, energetic and decisive measures of that indomitable Jackson whom men, for his toughness and his integrity, loved to call "Old Hickory."

Spain's power was weakening. Across the boundary, lured on by hope of booty, there swarmed in the spring of 1817 that motley crowd of picturesque adventurers and piratical tramps self-styled the "Patriot Army of the Republics of New Granada and Venezuela." With a name that meant nothing but a cover for rascality, as lawless as they were irresponsible, this crowd of old-time "boomers" burst across the Spanish borders and forced the timorous commandant to lower the flag of his king before their insolent demands.

The government of the United States, unwilling to allow a band of desperadoes to occupy, lawfully or unlawfully, by conquest or otherwise, any portion of the land that should be American only, sent troops into Florida, drove out the questionable "Patriots" and took possession of the country.

Following this came the Seminole trouble of 1818. An Indian outbreak that scarcely rose above the dignity of a savage foray it was openly fostered by British influence and winked at by Spanish incompetency.

Then it was that Jackson with a slender army of invasion marched against the Indians. With his sharpshooters and his home-raised militia he fell upon the red-men, burned their villages, drove them into the swamps and morasses of the lower peninsula, captured and hung the British agents and taking possession of the last Spanish post of Pensacola sent the garrison flying across the water to Havana. It was an act of usurpation as high-handed as it was patriotic. But, in periods of great public danger, might is ever esteemed as right, and Jackson's energetic measures saved the southern border from pillage and made Florida forever American.

This was in 1818. In 1821 Florida passed by sale and treaty into the possession of the United States. Once an American territory settlement grew. The American settler has always been restless under restrictions. Seeking to conquer the forest and the plain with axe and plough, he has always held as an enemy those earlier red possessors of the soil to whom axe and plough have ever been but the hated instruments of the white men's hated ways. From the days of the earliest colonization this hostility has burned or smouldered according to opportunity and every acre of border cultivation has been won only in the face of bitter opposition or of open "outrage" on the part of the Indian. The occupation of Florida proved no exception to the rule. Inch by inch the Indians in the north of the flowery peninsula were pressed into the swamps, the forests and the fastnesses of the south. Protest led to recrimination; to this succeeded open hostilities. In 1835 Indian retaliation broke out into warfare and a United States military force, comprising fourteen companies of regular troops, was dispatched against

JACKSON'S SHARPSHOOTERS.

the Florida Indians. Force and ferocity met face to face and the government of the United States had upon its hands that series of battles and conflicts known to history as the Florida or "Seminole" War.

This was no new experience either to government or army.

Already in the west a still more formidable because better organized Indian war had been met, grappled with and forced to a successful termination. In 1827 the Winnebagoes of Illinois had risen against the occupation of their land by the lead miners of Galena and joining to themselves the still more warlike Sioux plunged the country into war. The miners were formed into companies and equipped for action. Illinois volunteers hurried to the scene of trouble and six hundred United States regulars were added to the army. The Winnebago War was of short duration. The show of force brought by the authorities speedily overawed the hostile savages and the poor Winnebagoes, as many another Indian has done, before and since, abandoned their prairies to the greedy grasp of the white man. The only noble figure that stands out against the background of this little war cloud is that of the noble Sioux chieftain Red Bird who, when the Winnebagoes whom he had incited to hostility were pressed into defeat by the victorious white men, offered himself as the voluntary sacrifice for those whom he would not desert. Robed in skins and bearing a white flag, he rode into the United States camp and surrendered himself a voluntary prisoner with the spirit of one who though conquered was yet a conqueror. To the shame of American justice it must be said that this heroic "savage" was, without compunction, thrown into prison where he sickened and died of the humiliation of restraint.

But out of this Winnebago war rose speedily the greater and much more serious trouble known as the Black Hawk War. That celebrated Indian patriot known to the white men as Black Hawk, the chief of the Sacs, had allied himself with the Winnebagoes, had suffered imprisonment at the hands of the white conquerors and was filled with resentment against the settlers because of this indignity and because of the persistent encroachments of the white men upon the lands of his tribe. Removed under protest to the region beyond the Mississippi he chafed under this action and as soon as the military were withdrawn he returned to the Illinois country with a band of warriors as determined as was he. There on the fourteenth of May, 1832, he fell upon the United States soldiers on Sycamore Creek and defeated them with considerable loss. The settlers flew to arms. General Winfield Scott was assigned to the command and hastened westward with one thousand regulars to the assistance of the border volunteers who had taken the field against the redoubtable Indian chieftain. The war of course could have but one issue. In all the history of Indian warfare in America the final victory has always been vouchsafed to the white men; but before that victory had been attained the conflict had known, as well on the savage as on the civilized side, many an instance of courage and valor, of self-sacrifice and renown, of cruelty and cowardice. Black Hawk was a born warrior. A Kentuckian and therefore an Indian hater, in his story of the action of Sycamore Creek referred to above, asserted that the Indian army came against them not in the old-style skulking way of the savage but in solid column, deploying in the form of a crescent upon the borders of the prairie and with accuracy and precision in every movement. It must be said of this same Kentuckian private that perhaps his eyes played him false as his heart certainly did, for when the battle was joined he became a sadly-demoralized fighter. As the Indian attack fell upon his column he confesses that he made a retrograde movement and remained some time meditating what further he could do in the service of his country. "Then a random ball came whistling by my ear and whispered to me: 'Stranger, you have no further business here.'" Upon hearing this, he confesses, he followed the example of his companions in arms " and broke for the tall timber, and the way I ran was not a little."

But there were those who did not run. The war was prosecuted with firmness and energy on the part of the United States, with obstinacy and determination by Black Hawk and his followers. The battle of the Wisconsin however as the first decisive battle of the war threw the advantage and the victory into the hands of the Americans. The battle of the Bad Axe, fought on the second of August, 1832, drove the Indians into the Mississippi and defeat.

There never has been a war on American soil, since first the republic was proclaimed, that did not exhibit certain phases of that never-ending jealousy that has always seemed to exist between the regulars and the militia. Even in this Black Hawk War — a local disturbance only so far as the country at large was concerned — the success of the Illinois militia under General Henry, "the hero of the Wisconsin" as his own people loved to call him, was belittled by the officers of the regular army and over-laughed by Henry's own fellow officers who were jealous of their comrade's brilliant success. Honor to whom honor is due; and even at this late day it would seem but a slight acknowledgment of duty done and valor displayed to give alike the credit and the honor of the Black Hawk Campaign to the volunteers of the western border and to their energetic commander General James B. Henry whose intrepidity and good judgment turned defeat into victory in the battle of the Wisconsin and ended the war at Bad Axe.

Although General Scott did not actually assume command of the army in the Black Hawk War until after Henry and

Alexander had practically closed the campaign, the trouble was virtually concluded under his direction and when the Seminole trouble in Florida, in 1835, assumed serious proportions he was dispatched to the front by the War Department with a considerable and well-organized army. It was largely under his direction that the Florida war was waged.

From the start this war was fought out by the Indians with divided counsels. It sprang originally from an alleged infraction of treaty and leading chiefs of the Seminoles were still inclined to adhere to their promises as made under the treaty. The Seminole war was therefore not directly due to the leading Indians but was fostered and kept alive by the unyielding hatred and persistence of one man — Asseola (mistakenly called Osceola) the half-breed. Compounded of many diverse elements, with a character that was in many respects alien to Indian life and laws, Asseola added to the obstinacy of the Scotchman the worst traits of the red-man, and the Florida war was one long record of treacheries, inhumanities, surprises and dogged determination that, to a certain extent, explains how, in so narrow a strip of country as is the Florida peninsula, hostilities could be kept alive for nearly seven years.

The courage of the soldiers sent to the war by the settlers of the South and by the War Department was high; their desires for deeds of prowess were strong; but the fight was a long and wasting one and was based upon the customary Indian tactics of predatory forays, ambush and secrecy. The bravery of the soldier could only be shown in his continual wariness, his ability to ferret out the hiding foeman, his resort to stratagem and decoy, and his facing the Indian obstinacy with that higher persistence and determination with which intelligence always confronts savagery.

From 1835 to 1842 the war dragged on. Gaines, Scott, Call, Jesup, Taylor and Armistead each, in turn, succeeded to the general command or were superseded in it. The trouble was finally brought to a close after the expenditure of many lives and a large sum of money by that dashing soldier whose valor was to be even more severely tested on the plains of Mexico — General Thomas Worth. He succeeded to the command of the army in Florida in 1841. Conqueror in an active campaign, he penetrated into the inaccessible swamps and fastnesses where the Seminoles had taken refuge, forced them to a final surrender and to a removal to the far West. Already in 1836 Asseola the half-breed had been captured by stratagem and fraud and thrown into prison never to emerge alive. And thus another chapter in the sad story of the hopelessness of savage patriotism was written in blood and loss.

As typical of the Indian determination and the American persistence which, as has already been said, joined issue in this Seminole War, and as presenting all the varying phases of surprise and strategy, of ferocity and revenge, must ever stand the terrible story of that heroic defense made in the swamps of the Withlacoochee by Major Dade and his brave one hundred.

Ambushed and attacked by a strong party of savages on the morning of the twenty-eighth of December, 1835, while changing camp north of the Little Withlacoochee the troops quickly recovered from their surprise and charged the hidden foe. Beneath the thin shadow of the palmettoes where a stretch of high Southern grass almost concealed the skulking enemy the combatants met and fought hand to hand. Scalping knife and bayonet, clubbed musket and murderous hatchet clashed in the death grapple and even before the red-men had been driven back, Major Dade fell dead. His successor Captain Gardiner at once proceeded to throw up a slender breastwork which should serve as a slight obstacle to the assaults of the Indians again gathering for the attack. Before the feeble defense had risen to the height of two and a half feet the Indians, now largely reinforced, swarmed down upon the gallant little band. The yells of the savages drowned the noise of the muskets. In large numbers they surrounded that frail breastwork and shot down every man who attempted to serve the one gun that was its sole defense. Officer after officer was killed. At last only one remained. This was Lieutenant Bassinger. As he saw the last one above him in rank fall beneath the murderous fire he called out pluckily, "I'm the only officer left, boys; but we'll all do the best we can."

Poor fellows! their best was but to die bravely. And that they did. A fair prototype of that later day when on Western plains the brave fellows of Custer's command went down to a man, so now the forlorn hope of the gallant Dade stood valiantly to their work and the fight ended only when life and ammunition gave out together. Over the frail inclosure burst the victorious savages but there were no defenders left. Every man in that brave little company save one who managed to escape with the tidings of defeat, lay dead or dying within the space of their defenses. And when the Indians had taken their customary toll of scalps and departed, the runaway negroes who had sided with the Indians—a step lower down in savagery than were their red allies—completed the work of slaughtering the defenseless and pillaging the dead. But no indignity could efface the glory of that day's heroism. The valor of defeat is sometimes more deathless than is the jubilee shout of triumph.

The Black Hawk campaign and the Seminole War were the leading military events of that era of national peace that bridged the years between the treaty of Ghent and the war with Mexico. And yet within that time there were rumors of war forever in the air, there were internal disturbances that kept the War Department ever on the alert.

Most serious of all these internal dissensions, in its possible results (although the determined stand of one man stamped sternly out the incipient revolt which his over-sternness had nearly brought about), were the "Nullification Troubles" of 1832 when South Carolina, enraged at President Jackson's position upon the question of State rights, sought to nullify certain customs laws passed by Congress and openly defied the power of the United States.

The same stern sense of duty, the same inflexible courage that had broken the Creek confederacy at Horse Shoe Bend, that had hurled back the army of Packenham from the mud breastworks before New Orleans and had sent the Spaniards flying from Pensacola again asserted themselves and could find in the defiant position of a hot-headed Southern State only a greater incentive to patriotism, only the demand for a justice that must be inexorable. Andrew Jackson was not a man to yield.

"By the Eternal!" the stout old soldier-president declared in one of his favorite explosives, "the Union must and shall be preserved. Send for General Scott!"

Quick to respond to the call of his country General Scott came and, with most of the available troops of the United States army, he was hurried at once to the city of Charleston, the center of the threatened insurrection.

But though the military of the State was duly ordered out to repel the "invaders" the determined stand of the stout old hero of New Orleans had almost instant effect. Defiance changed to compliance, and this earliest attempt of a State to revolt against the nation of which it was a component part was itself "nullified" by the unyielding patriotism of that nation's chief executive and by the bristling bayonets of that nation's regular soldiery.

The country was growing rapidly. A ceaseless flow of immigration was changing the forests into farm lands, the prairies into pastures and wheat-fields. But growth implies unrest and the three decades between 1815 and 1845 were marked with vain attempts at hostility or by vague rumors of trouble that never came. East, west and south this spirit of unrest repeatedly appeared and the ill effects of intrigue in politics or diplomacy seemed continually to threaten a contest.

Now it was the Mormons who were reported to be aiming to subvert the institutions and the religion of the land. Against them the people protested even to the verge of open assault and both the destruction of Nauvoo in Illinois and the anti-Mormon riots in Missouri called for the service of the soldiers of those States to scatter the militant sect.

Again it was that outbreak of 1842 in Rhode Island known as Dorr's Rebellion — a protest unjustly derided, the real history of which is yet to be written — that called the fighting men to arms; or it was that serio-comic "invasion of Canada" in 1839 when seven hundred restless New Yorkers led by a descendant of the patroons of Rensselaer offered themselves as allies and supporters of a Canadian revolt against England, and the troops of the United States were hurried northward to enforce American neutrality and protect the disturbed frontiers. There were many local disturbances such as the "Anti-rent war" in New York and the "Bank mobs" in Maryland that demanded the service of the military arm to scatter or punish while even the political party cry of the presidential campaign of 1844: "fifty-four forty or fight!" — a demand for northwestern boundaries that threatened a third war with England — filled the land with anxiety and fired the hearts of those ambitious for military glory.

These and such as these, however serious, however ridiculous they might be, created, each, a certain demand for resistance by a show of force that should summon either the scattered ranks of the slender regular army or the uncertain files of an all-too uncertain militia. In a free country the citizen is not inclined to do anything more than play at soldier until a real and stern demand calls him to duty and often to death.

From a very early day, however, this playing at soldier has held an important place in American life. As early as 1666 the colonial laws required all males among the colonists to attend military exercises and services. Companies were exercised six days annually, the captain opening every such training with prayer. The law of 1790 required every able-bodied male between the ages of eighteen and forty-five to meet with his military company four times each year for training and discipline and the United States law of 1792 sought to establish a general militia system throughout the entire country. The Revolution had given a new impetus to the martial spirit; the imbecilities of 1812 gave it a spasmodic growth; and thus through the first half of the present century the "general training" and the muster day of the spring and fall were the red letter days of the year in all American towns. Let us for a moment, dear reader, be the "Father and I" of that rattling old jingle that has now become historic — those two spectators who, say, in the early twenties or even in the early thirties

> Went down to camp
> Along with Cap'n Gooding,
> And there we saw the men and boys
> As thick as hasty-pudding."

They are thick hereabouts and no mistake. People everywhere. And as Cap'n Gooding leaves us and we shake from our shoes the dust of the dry road along which we have plodded to the camp we stand now upon the broad green or "Common" just beyond the limits of the county town. The field is flanked with peddler's wagons and with booths and stands of every description hastily knocked together for " this day only." Muster day is a great incentive to inordinate appetite for indigestible stuffs and both at the town tavern close at hand and here in this encircling encampment of booths and wagons everything deemed most palatable in the way of eatables and drinkables is offered for sale alike to citizen and soldier.

The shrill fife and the roll of drum call the soldiers to their stations. And now the regiment gathers together — a sight to behold. We stand on tiptoe to view the muster and the evolutions, for these are the days of simplicity in the republic and no such aristocratic luxuries as grand stands or tiers of seats are provided for the spectators. The regiment embraces the four divisions of the military service — artillery, grenadiers, light infantry, and riflemen with a dash of cavalry to add excitement to the scene. Here, too, come the ununiformed raw recruits known as the "floodwood companies."

The spectators are all agog. They are full of admiration for the cavalrymen, mounted on horses of every degree of mettle and decked out in black suits faced, and corded with red. These sit astride their cumbrous saddles terrible with clanking cutlasses and formidable holsters into which are thrust the huge horse pistols of that ante-revolver day. The red leather helmets of the grenadiers gleam in the hot sun. Soft hats are as yet a thing unknown and the stiff black beavers of the riflemen in their quiet uniform of gray, and the black leather cap of the infantry, topped each with a black and red feather are as comfortless as they are unpicturesque. The infantry we shall look at again and again. Theirs is the most gorgeous of uniform. It is composed of white trousers and black coats the latter criss-crossed with white belts to which are chained priming wires, brushes and extra flints. The "floodwood" men are, as a rule, innocent of uniform. Only a tin badge displayed in the front of their hat and bearing the letters L. I. tells us that these undecorated recruits (who generally outnumber the uniformed companies two to one) are really martial members of the Light Infantry of the State. They are a prosaic patch in a field of color.

The color would seem to be the only picturesque element however, for the art of military tailoring was of a low grade in the twenties and thirties. Thoreau once said, "Wrap a salt-fish around a boy and he would have a coat much in the fashion of many a one I have seen worn at muster."

And now comes inspection. The dull lines of the "floodwoods" (sober in their sheep's gray and blue jeans and armed with rifles, muskets and fowling pieces of every conceivable pattern) are ordered to "toe the mark" — a literal mark literally toed. Man by man the platoons are inspected and then along the line rides the Colonel and his staff, resplendent in brass buttons, big epaulets and vast cocked hats. The music crashes out. It is more voluminous than harmonious for the instruments have come from all the towns about. Its only uniformity is its tendency to play out of tune. With a roll and a rattle the snare and kettle-drums burst out; boom! go the basses and high and shrill rise the notes of fife and clarionet, with here and there, perhaps, a Kent bugle — the father of the cornet. Still clashing out of tune the band gathers around the colonel while the regiment forms itself into a hollow square. And the colonel doffing his chapeau, poses like the great Napoleon and after addressing a few complimentary words to his faithful regiment retires from the field.

Inspection over, dinner follows. Then the noon gun calls the regiment back to the parade ground where each company tries to outdo the others in a competitive drill and evolutions the movements of which are all unknown to modern tactics.

A break in the maneuvers is caused by those who, lacking cartridges, cannot, to the letter, obey the command: "Open pan; tear cartridge; point; shut pan; ram down cartridge! Ready! Aim! Fire!" Each cartridge-less one must go down into his breeches pocket for the well-filled powder-flask from which to prime his pan. And more than one unfortunate in the excitement of the moment, explodes his magazine in his capacious pocket and retires from the field singed and scorched — wrecked in whiskers, hair or eyebrows.

Or perhaps the captain shouts "Lock-step and sit down!" Then in single file the company march about, forming a circle in the center of which stands the captain. To slow music the circle draws toward the center falling into the "lock-step" now only known to convict gangs. "Sit!" cries the captain, and down goes each man in the lap of his neighbor — for all the world like a company of leap-frogs preparing to jump. In the center, perched high on a mackerel keg, stands the valiant captain with uplifted sword; the music rises shrill and high and the admiring spectators wildly applaud the tableau.

And now comes what the crowd consider the great event of the day — the sham battle. In a rudely constructed house of

IN THE "ANTI-RENT WAR."

boards and boughs, excluding air and light and supposed to represent a fort, one of the militia companies huddles imprisoned. Advancing by platoons the infantry men of the regiment march upon the fort, discharge their guns in air, wheel outward and retire to re-load. From the top of a neighboring hill boom out the blank charges of the artillery — a battery of bloodless besiegers. Still farther away the black coats of the cavalry charge and swerve in a sham fight on their own account. The air is filled with noise and smoke until the sweltering defenders of the fort, overcome by heat, rather than by heroism, gladly capitulate and marching out with all the honors of war give place in the fort to another company who immediately take possession of it, likewise to swelter and surrender.

And when the sham fight is over the day's training at last is done. "Father and I" leave the field and return with Cap'n Gooding convinced that a muster is a grand and glorious sight.

And yet, notwithstanding this semi-annual exercise and evolution, it is asserted that in all those early days there was scarcely a company of militia-men really well drilled or proficient in even the most simple military movement.

Practically the United States were at peace from the close of the War of 1812 to the opening of the war with Mexico in 1846. Military duties were slighted and shirked by the majority of Americans who could poorly spare any of the precious time necessary to the noble science of money-making for such "fol-de-rols" as muster and parade. Gradually, so great was the contempt visited upon "belonging to the military" that the militia system itself fell into disrepute and became a butt and a reproach. That typical raw recruit of the Biglow Papers, "Mr. Birdofredom Sawin," was, we know, ceaselessly critical of the fuss and feathers of muster day. Real war when he had to face it, he declared,

> "ain't a mite like our October trainin',
> A chap could clear right out from there ef 't only looked like rainin',
> An' th' Cunnles, tu, could kiver up their shappoes with bandanners,
> An' send the insines skootin' to the bar-room with their banners
> (Fear o' gittin' on 'em spotted), an' a feller could cry quarter
> Ef he fired away his ramrod arter tu much rum an' water."

The "forced volunteers" of the West—men drafted to serve in the militia of a State in which they had neither time nor desire to serve—not unfrequently protested against discipline and proscription. So the militia system gradually fell into disrepute. In a land where caste and rank find but little footing and where social distinctions are of small account obedience in playing at war is but a grudging, a contemptuous or a good-humored concession.

"See here, Brown," a militia officer is said to have called out to one of the privates (who when at home, was the pompous captain's employer). "I reckon I'll have to report you for disrespect to your superior officer."

"Report and be hanged!" returned the private, with no little emphasis in his tone. "When we get home I reckon I'll have to discharge you."

President Lincoln once stated that, previous to the Mexican war, so great a bore did militia trainings become to the people of Illinois that they tried in every way to put them down. Not being able to do this by repealing the militia laws they tried hard to burlesque them. And so, according to Mr. Lincoln's story, they elected one Gordon Adams, a village "bummer" and ne'er-do-well, as colonel of a Springfield regiment. The new colonel's uniform, contributed by his subordinates, was truly startling. One leg of his trousers was of one color and material, the other was in direct contrast. He wore a pasteboard cap about six feet long, looking much like an inverted ox-yoke. The shanks of his spurs were fully eight inches long and furnished with rowels as big as saucers. His sword was of pine wood and at least nine feet long. Among the regimental rules and regulations were incorporated certain absurd clauses, as for instance this: "No officer shall wear

CARICATURING THE MILITIA.
President Lincoln's story of "Colonel" Gordon Adams.

more than twenty pounds of codfish for epaulets, nor more than thirty yards of Bologna sausage for a sash." Upon the regimental banner was borne aloft these words: "We'll fight till we run and run till we die." The appearance of "Colonel" Adams according to Mr. Lincoln's narrative ended militia training in Springfield. It was killed by caricature!

A certain Indiana major, filled with an importance of the pomp and circumstance of mimic war as embodied in "general training" day and his own ability to lead was once elected to command in a Wayne County regiment. He was not an imposing figure. He had, so the record declares, "like Julius Cæsar, a weak body but the military ambition of a Charles the Twelfth." What he lacked in stature he sought to make up in uniform. The muster day arrived. The adjutant spurred from the headquarters and with a loud voice issued his orders: "Officers, to your places. Marshal your men into companies. Separate the barefooted from those wearing shoes or moccasins; place the guns, sticks and corn-stalks in separate platoons, and form in line to receive the major!"

The line was formed and then, into the field, amid the clash of music, dashed the major and his aids. The little officer was almost lost in his gorgeous uniform. He wore a blue coat, covered with gold lace and big gilt buttons; upon his head was a chapeau, copied after Jackson's at the Horse Shoe fight, above which towered a red plume tipped with white. Great epaulets weighed down his narrow shoulders; his sword-scabbard reached to his feet; his legs were cased in Suwarrow boots that over-topped his pistol-stuffed holster and were graced with gilt spurs fully a foot long. Facing the waiting regiment the little major reined in his rearing horse, rose in his stirrups and shouted bravely: "Attention, the whole!"

But, alas! his voice was weak. It broke on the "Attention!" It rose into a fifelike squeak on "the whole." And just then from the extreme end of the regimental line came piping back an exact imitation of the major's squeak: "Chillun! Come out 'er the swamp. You'll get snake-bit!"

Down the line dashed the enraged major. "Who dares insult me?" he demanded with fury in his eyes. And for reply there came all along the line the same mocking squeak: "Snake-bit; snake-bit; you'll get snake-bit!"

Mortified and angered beyond endurance the poor little major's assumption of pomp and ceremony fell to dust and ashes. He dashed his chapeau from his head; he flung his sword to the ground; he tore his commission to pieces and resigned his office on the spot. There was no recovery from so open a farce and the last militia muster had been held in the White Water country.

On a certain "trainin'" day in New Hampshire a fuss-and-feathers captain ordered the double-quick. Away dashed the command but presently the captain, throwing a glance over his shoulder to note the effect of the maneuver was thunderstruck to find himself running alone. Going back to hunt up his missing company he found them, over the fence — chasing chickens!

Down in Virginia the captain of a militia company fell into hot dispute with his adjutant on training day. The whole parade was demoralized. Just as the war of words rose hottest a three-hundred pound hog, worried by the dogs, dashed across the parade ground and darting between the legs of the angry captain sent him sprawling to the ground. With shrieks of laughter and loud hand-clapping soldiers and citizens applauded the overthrow. But springing to his feet the doughty captain tore off his military coat, with all its entangling straps and belts, flung aside his sword and rolling up his shirt sleeves, shouted out in a fury: "Come on, you! I'll lick the whole company!" The tall file leader who stood nearest him, "bent like a willow-wand" in the brawny captain's grasp. Such valor was not to be disputed. Awed by their captain's physical powers more than by his "panoply of war" the company was re-formed and the mutiny was quelled.

But if the militia in those "piping times of peace" was a crude, unorganized and graceless sort of body — a very emphasis, in fact, of the unwarlike character of the American people when nothing urges them to conflict — the eight thousand soldiers who made up the slender regular army were carefully drilled and thoroughly organized. Hampered by many restrictions and enwrapped in much departmental red tape, it was yet officered by men who, learning a lesson from the failures of 1812, resolved never again to permit the army of the United States to be a stumbling block and a reproach.

Gallant officers and rigid disciplinarians, such men as Brown, Macomb and Scott, were generals of the army between the years 1815 and 1846. Their vigor, their energy and their determination to give to the service strength and standing, put into soldierly training the little force at whose head in turn they stood, and educated men and officers alike to be ready for efficient service in the two years' war that was fast drawing near.

CHAPTER IX.

OVER THE MEXICAN BORDER.

MEXICO—land of sunlight and of shadow, of peon and planter, of simplicity and superstition, of courtesy and cupidity, of lazy manners and of flaming passions — what spirit of evil could have induced a powerful northern nation to seek the humbling and the spoiling of so picturesque and yet so ambitious, so distracted and yet so devoted, so patriotic and yet so partisan a sister republic? Fired by the example of the Northern colonies in their revolt against English tryanny the land of the Aztecs had in 1815 declared itself independent and in 1821 had thrown off the yoke of Spain.

The republic of Mexico! Surely here was an effort toward progress and freedom worthy to be fostered and upheld by that great people whose success had given it being. What if it was torn by faction and jealousies, a hot-bed of revolutions and of unfulfilled opportunities? Ought it not to have been all the more a land to be befriended by a people who had conquered circumstances and obtained success? And yet in 1846 the northern eagles swooped down upon the southern doves and dyed the tricolored banner of Mexico in the blood of her bravest and her best.

It is not the province of this volume to enter into the causes of those various wars in which the American soldier has played his part. But it must be admitted that no conflict in which the republic of the United States had been one of the principals was ever more unnecessary, heartless or unjust. A little cool judgment on the part of our national leaders, a little friendly concession toward a weaker neighbor, a determined effort toward that arbitration which to-day is the great pacificator of the world — and the willful waste of blood and treasure, the shame and taint of our war against Mexico might never have sullied the name of the United States.

A war conceived in the interests of slavery, advocated as a political necessity and precipitated by the unwarranted occupation of a strip of foreign, or at least of neutral ground — such was the war with Mexico! No wonder our justice-loving Northern poet cried out in wrath

> "Where's now the flag of that old war?
> Where flows its stripe? Where burns its star?
> Bear witness, Palo Alto's day,
> Dark vale of Palms, red Monterey;
> Where Mexic freedom, young and weak,
> Fleshes the northern eagle's beak;
> Symbol of terror and despair,
> Of chains and slaves, go seek it there!"

And yet so incongruous is fate, so unreasoning is heroism, the very war that should have been distasteful to freemen — a war in behalf of oppression, offensive and not defensive, aggressive and not resistant, wrong and not right — this was the one war of all others, up to that stage of American history, most replete with daring, heroism and resistless successes. Fought, always, against fearful odds, in a strange land and in an unfriendly climate, from first to last the war was full of triumph for the stars and stripes. The march of the American soldiers across the Mexican borders and into the old Aztec capital was but one continuous series of victories.

The nation was ready for war. Schooled by the imbecilities and reverses of 1812 to an appreciation of military needs the regular army of the United States, as has already been said, though small in numbers was admirably drilled and yet more admirably officered. The military academy at West Point, founded by act of Congress in 1802, had been reorganized in 1812 and placed upon such a basis of excellence and effort that its graduates left it soldiers in training as well as in theory.

The men who led and who fought in the ranks of the United States army in 1846 and 1847, were men indeed,— picked from the fighting stock of a nation which, notwithstanding the farces of muster days and the empty pomp of "general training," had still at base the valor, the endurance and the pluck that was the heritage of that time that tried men's souls threescore years before — the outcome of those historic days when men rallied for the right and laid down their lives for Liberty.

Professor Soley, carefully studying the details of the Mexican war, asserts that "the skill and daring of the officers, and the discipline, endurance and courage of the men during the war with Mexico, were as noticeable as was the absence of these qualities during the War of 1812." Here was no leaderless war. The names of Taylor and of Scott, of Worth and Wool, of Quitman and Kearney, of McKenzie and Shields belonged alike to leaders and to soldiers and, in the lack of competent Mexican generals, afford one reason for the unvarying successes of the American arms.

The determined efforts of Texas (largely settled by Americans) to free itself from the Mexic-Spanish yoke, the heroic stand at the Alamo — that "Thermopylæ of America" — the dreary tragedy of Goliad, the valorous and triumphant conflict at San Jacinto lost the Lone Star republic to Mexico, brought her at last into the confederation of the United States and aroused the world to a fresh sympathy with brave men nerved to heroic endeavor by a great desire. What man with fighting blood in his veins or the inspiration of courage in his heart would not be stirred to admiration by the heroism of Travis and his brave two hundred and fifty at the Alamo and by the desperate valor of San Houston's eight hundred at San Jacinto? Valor begets enthusiasm, and when at last war against Mexico was declared there was but little reasoning among those who saw, in the fight over a new empire, opportunity for great deeds and martial experiences. To him who longed to shoulder a musket or swing a saber the question as to right or wrong counted for but little. The invasion of Mexico might be "a political necessity," the contest might be only a "war of pretext" — both invasion and contest afforded, at least, a pretext for valorous deeds, a necessity for sturdy fighters and, to the soldiers, these were as all in all.

So off to the wars they marched — regulars and volunteers alike, all filled with a desire for action, all swayed with the hope of glory. Their general was that Zachary Taylor whose army nickname of "Old Rough and Ready" sufficiently indicates his character. Rough indeed he was when warlike necessities called for vigorous actions; and ready, too, the record shows him to have been whether responding to the government's call for the immediate occupation of the disputed territory or storming against the host of foeman below the rocky heights that frowned on Angostura.

Seizing the disputed stretch of territory that lay, two hundred miles in width, along the eastern bank of the Rio Grande, General Taylor with his Army of Occupation, twenty-five hundred strong, rendezvoused at Point Isabel not far from the mouth of the Great River. His force comprised one thousand regulars and less than fifteen hundred volunteers drawn from the southwestern States. It consisted of one regiment of cavalry ("dragoons"), four companies of light artillery, five regiments of infantry and one regiment of artillery acting as infantry. Over the camp at Point Isabel floated the American flag and this was deemed by the Mexicans alike an insult and an invitation to war. And war began.

The Mexican bombardment of Fort Brown, a hastily constructed fortification thrown up by the Americans on the banks of the river opposite Matomoras, was the signal for battle. The battle followed speedily. It was a double engagement fought with all the faith that comes from superiority of numbers by the over-confident Mexicans and with all the valor of desperation by the little American army. Along the easterly side of the Rio Grande North and South met in conflict. In this double fight — the battles of Palo Alto and Resaca de la Palma, in both of which the Mexican array of over six thousand men outnumbered the Americans almost three to one — the courage of the northern army and the ability of its leader stood the test of battle and gave the key-note to this epic of war. A five hours' fight at Palo Alto — the "tall trees" — on the eighth of May gave the victory to the Northern arms. On the ninth the yet fiercer fight at Resaca de la Palma sent the Mexicans flying across the river in full retreat and the first victory was won. The Mexican contempt for their Northern antagonists was changed to consternation. With one seventh of their number wounded or prisoners, the Mexican soldiers fled before the northern bayonet, enraged yet defeated and as one American officer has testified "throwing their muskets at our men in the spirit of desperation, swearing that they were devils incarnate." It was a sad revelation to the too-confident Mexicans. The victory they so unquestioningly expected was but bitter defeat. The wail of disaster lives in the lines of one of their native poets:

> "Dark is Palo Alto's story,
> Sad Resaca Palma's rout;
> On those fatal fields so gory
> Many a gallant life went out.
>
> "On they came, those Northern horsemen,
> On like eagles through the sun;
> Followed then the Northern bayonet,
> And the field was lost and won."

The field indeed was lost and won. General Taylor crossed the Rio Grande. The Army of Occupation became the Army of Invasion. The effect of these battles on the American people was like an elixir. It fired them to ambitious and determined action. The president issued a call for fifty thousand volunteers. Ten times that number responded. The Government could not handle the host and only the number called for was sent south. It was divided into three sections — the Army of Occupation, the Army of the Center and the Army of the West. Sixty-five hundred men shouldered their flint-locks and at once the forward march was taken for this modern conquest of Mexico.

It is characteristic of human nature to honor heroism and to emphasize, in the story of a successful war, not the blood but the bravery that it displays. As the years go by and the real horrors of conflict and carnage are weakened by remoteness so are the valorous deeds intensified and made to appear gleaming and glorious.

The triumphal march on Mexico made by the American soldiers takes to itself as we now look back upon it all the glitter and romance of the historic deeds of those old *conquistadores* of Spain who, amid these same hills and valleys, turned a race of progressive barbarians into a nation of slaves. Alvarado's mighty leap across the broken causeway, Sandoval's dashing charge up the bloody stairway of the Aztec temple and Olid's fiery valor at Otumba are recalled by May's terrific charge upon the Mexican batteries at Resaca de la Palma, by Smith's furious onset at Contreras and by Quitman's stubborn defense of the San Belen gate.

And as we are apt, in the glamour of Spanish victory, to lose sight of the bravery of those heroic *tzins* of the Aztec — Cacama and Guatamo — so we place in our records of this modern conquest but scant mention of that brave Mexican color-sergeant who on the stricken field of Palo Alto left the fight, the last of his regiment, wrapped in the folds of the flag he had so valiantly defended — the tattered banner of the Tampico Veterans; we find but brief reference to that gallant old Revolutionary leader Bravo and his young cadets of the Mexican military academy who held the hill of Chapultepec against the terrible charge of their Northern foeman. It is time for us to give up the old fable that the Mexicans who withstood our arms were only greasers and cowards. It is proper for us to bear in mind that in the Mexican calendar Cherubusco and Chapultepec are celebrated as victories instead of defeats — the birthdays of patriotism and valor. That these patriots were foemen worthy of our steel full many a northern soldier on those bloody fields learned to his cost.

"The Mexican army of that day," says General Grant, "was hardly an organization. The private soldier was poorly clothed, worse fed and seldom paid; yet I have seen as brave stands made by some of these men as I have ever seen made by soldiers."

Honoring those whose names gave emphasis to victory we read the record of this unnecessary but fascinating war with no little enthusiasm. Our caps are flung aloft at each recurring victory and we almost resent with indignation the grumbling criticisms of that same grumbling volunteer of the "Biglow Papers" who, after the war was over, declared with equally bad grace and bad grammar:

> "But somehow, wen we'd fit an' licked, I ollers found the thanks
> Got kin' o' lodged afore they come ez low down ez the ranks;
> The Gin'rals got the biggest sheer, the Cunnels next, an' so on, —
> We never got a blasted might o' glory ez I know on.
> An' s'pose we hed, I wonder how you 're goin' to contrive its
> Division so's to give a piece to twenty thousand privits;
> Ef you should multiply by ten the portion o' the brav'st one,
> You wouldn't git mor'n half enough to speak of on a gravestun;
> We git the licks — we're jest the grist thet's put into War's hoppers;
> Leftenants is the lowest grade thet helps pick up the coppers.
> It may suit folks thet go agin a body with a soul in 't;
> An' ain't contented with a hide without a baguet hole in 't;
> But glory is a kin' o' thing I sha'n't pursue no furder,
> Coz thet's the off'cers parquisite, — yourn's on'y jest the murder."

Looked at from the standpoint of right the war against Mexico was unwarranted, unnecessary and inexcusable; regarded from the standpoint of action it was thrilling, inspiring and glorious. Inch by inch through a hostile country, against a myriad odds, with an enemy outnumbering it many times over, the American army pushed on from assault to assault and from victory to victory until the stars and stripes waved in triumph above the halls of the Montezumas. The valor at Palo Alto, the dogged determination at Resaca de la Palma formed but the proem to this epic of war. The only time in its history that the United States invaded a foreign country the story of that invasion is one unbroken record of daring and success.

The bloody streets of Monterey, the smoked-filled defiles of Buena Vista, the echoing batteries of Vera Cruz, the stricken tower of Cerro Gordo, the ragged lava beds of Contreras, the fated fortress of Cherubusco, the shattered structure of Molino Del Rey, the storied height of Chapultepec, the battered gates of Mexico alike bore terrible evidence of the stubbornness and bravery, the valor and the resistless sweep of that little army of Northern invaders who, at every step, forced victory out of desperate chances and sowed the seeds of an international enmity that not forty years of peace have yet removed. The war with Mexico retrieved the imbecilities of 1812 and raised the name of the American soldier to a place of glory and honor that found its after fruits in the desperate life struggle of the nation where valor met valor, as brother grappled with brother on Virginian battle-fields and on the banks of the mighty Mississippi.

It was a war to make the philanthropist shudder and the soldier loudly huzza. Whittier's glimpse of the terrible battle of Buena Vista is not all romance and poetry; it is a picture of passion photographed by philanthropy:

> "Look forth once more, Ximena! 'Ah! the smoke has rolled away;
> And I see the Northern rifles gleaming down the ranks of gray.
> Hark! that sudden blast of bugles! there the troop of Minon wheels;
> There the Northern horses thunder, with the cannon at their heels.
>
> "'Jesu, pity! how it thickens! now retreat and now advance!
> Right against the blazing cannons shivers Puebla's charging lance!
> Down they go, the brave young riders; horse and foot together fall,
> Like a ploughshare in the fallow, through them ploughs the Northern ball.'
>
> . . . .
>
> "Look forth once more, Ximena! 'Like a cloud before the wind
> Rolls the battle down the mountains, leaving blood and death behind;
> Ah! they plead in vain for mercy; in the dust the wounded strive;
> Hide your faces, holy angels! O thou Christ of God, forgive!'
>
> "Sink, O Night, among thy mountains, let the cool gray shadows fall,
> Dying brothers, fighting demons, drop thy curtain over all!
> Through the thickening winter twilight, wide apart the battle rolled,
> In its sheath the saber rested, and the cannon's lips grew cold.
>
> "Not wholly lost, O Father! is this evil world of ours;
> Upward, through its blood and ashes, spring afresh the Eden flowers;
> From its smoking hell of battle, Love and Pity send their prayer,
> And still thy white winged angels hover dimly in our air!'"

There are triumphs of brain quite as marvelous as those of muscle; there are victories of strategy more complete than those of sword and bayonet. Such was Taylor's masterly retreat from Agua Nueva by which was secured the wonderful victory of Buena Vista; such, too, was that shrewd change of base by which Scott avoided the trap set for him by the wily Santa Anna and opened the way for his almost unresisted march upon the Mexican capital.

And, as typical of those displays of valor in which generalship overcame numbers and brute force yielded to discipline, none of the engagements of the war stand out with greater distinctness than does the victory at Buena Vista and that desperate fight which waged near the convent at Cherubusco, won the way to Mexico.

In both engagements the Mexicans outnumbered the Americans almost four to one; but Buena Vista was fought almost under the shadows of that uncertainty as to the real fighting-qualities of Mexico's legions and the real persistence of America's bayonets which not even the valor of Palo Alto and Resaca de la Palma nor all the bloody memories of the determined fury at Monterey could yet quite remove; Cherubusco was almost the last of that unbroken series of victories that had, by that time, made America over-confident and Mexico despondent.

Pressing through the narrow defiles of those high Sierras that flank the open table-lands of Northern Mexico came, rank after rank, on the twenty-second of February, 1847, the army of Santa Anna, twenty thousand strong. Encamped upon a circumscribed plateau, that commanded the approaches upon every side, the little force of General Taylor, a scant five thousand men, awaited the onset of the foe. The army of the stout old American commander had been shorn of half its fighting strength, taken for the reinforcement of Scott's new army that was to march upon Mexico from the sea. This demand had withdrawn from Taylor's army, already small enough for operations in a hostile country, nearly all of the regulars, Worth's volunteers and Quitman's and Twiggs' commands. Enraged at the defeats in the north the Mexicans, in overwhelming numbers, had gathered under the lead of their wariest and most successful general to fall upon and utterly crush out this little remnant of northern invasion that had retreated from Agua

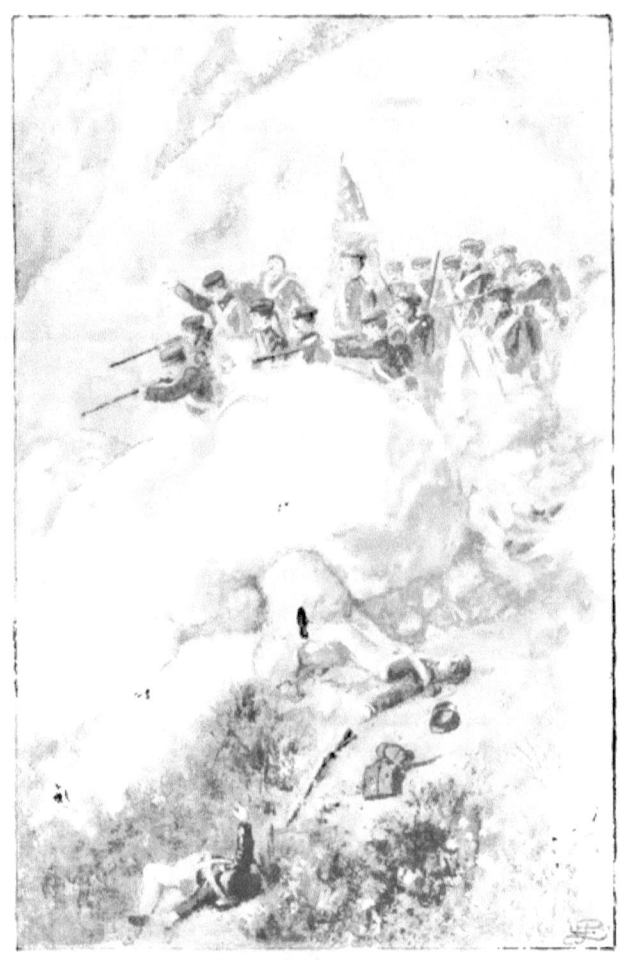

THE BATTLE OF BUENA VISTA.

"Down the hills of Angostura still the storm of battle rolls;
Blood is flowing, men are dying, God have mercy on their souls!"

Nueva and between whom and destruction there only waited the merciless order of the Mexican leader to slay and spare not. The situation was desperate indeed.

"You are surrounded by twenty thousand men," came the summons of Santa Anna to Taylor. "You cannot avoid being cut to pieces with your troops. Surrender at once and you shall be treated with that consideration that belongs to the Mexican character."

And back went the brief but plucky reply of "Old Rough and Ready:" "I decline to accede to your request."

Then Ampudia's light infantry rushed to the attack. The battle was joined:

> "Like the fierce northern hurricane
> That sweeps his great plateau,
> Flushed with the triumph yet to gain
> Came down the serried foe.
> Who heard the thunder of the fray
> Break o'er the field beneath
> Knew well the watchword of that day
> Was Victory or Death!"

But Ampudia's men fire wildly. The American riflemen are sure and steady of aim. And when the sun sank behind the overhanging hills the Americans still hold with stubborn determination the key to their position — La Angostura, "The Narrows," that pass of scanty width just south of the farm house of Buena Vista, through which the main portion of Santa Anna's army must push their way if they hope to gain the expected victory. And so night fell upon the field.

But the sun rose on a renewed struggle. Strongly reinforced, Ampudia's men drive in the American pickets. From five different positions the Mexicans press to the attack.

Destruction seems inevitable. The Indiana troops turn in flight, O'Brien's battery, deprived of its support, is overwhelmed and captured by the Mexican host it has so valiantly held at bay. The American left is turned. Fleeing soldiers rush wildly into Buena Vista crying that the day is lost.

But still the Americans hold the narrow pass. Charge as they will the men of Villamie's column cannot dislodge the little American battery that commands the roadway through the defile of Angostura. Victory trembles in the balance. Suddenly loud cheers ring out at Buena Vista and in a column of dust, spurring to the aid of his boys at bay in the Narrows, Old Rough and Ready comes riding from Saltillo where he has been arranging for the protection of his rear-guard.

"Never mind Villamie," he cried; "he's done for. Washington can hold the pass. Send the Mississippi riflemen to the left. Bring up the Third Indiana. Let Sherman's battery support them. May, ride with your dragoons to the upper plateau. Ampudia must be checked!"

And Ampudia was checked. The Mexican lancers, fifteen hundred strong, the special pride of Santa Anna, the flower of Mexico's army, go down like grain beneath the fire of the northern riflemen. The left is strengthened. The Mexicans, blind to the real key to the field, give over their assault on the Narrows. With a last mighty clash of arms the battle centers about the little hamlet of Buena Vista and almost before they know it the field is won.

The men of Kentucky and Arkansas bear back Ampudia's dashing cavalry. Forced backward, step by step, in a desperate hand-to-hand fight on horseback, go Torrejon and his dragoons. The commands of Ampudia and Pacheco, overwhelming in numbers are hemmed in between the narrow defiles and pounded at by three American batteries. Six thousand Mexicans are almost caught in a trap of their own making when a white flag flutters from the Mexican lines and Santa Anna coolly demands: "What does General Taylor want?"

The batteries cease firing, the troops rest for an armistice and the hemmed-in Mexicans escape from their trap. This at all events, is just what the wily Santa Anna wants; and when this is effected, clash! go his sabers; bang! go his guns again.

But not saber clash nor bang of gun can save the day for Mexico. Down in the dust before the pitiless grape and canister of O'Brien's batteries go Villamie's reserves; back to the hills flies the renegade brigade of San Patricio; Ampudia's men are in full retreat. Santa Anna himself, spent with this fruitless hurling of his masses against such undaunted men, gives up the battle with the sun. Night falls again upon Angostura and Buena Vista and, before morning dawns, the crippled Mexican army melt away and the stubborn fight of that twenty-third of February becomes the historic victory of Buena Vista — really the decisive battle of the war. Twenty-five hundred in killed and wounded, with four thousand missing and deserters is what Mexico paid for that dismal defeat; two hundred and sixty-four in killed, four hundred and fifty in wounded is the cost of America's triumph:

> "Full many a norther's breath has swept
>   O'er Angostura's plain,
> And long the pitying sky has wept
>   Above the mouldered slain.
> The raven's scream or eagle's flight,
>   Or shepherd's pensive lay,
> Alone now wakes each solemn height
>   That frowned on that dread fray."

Buena Vista was the key-note of victory in the north; in somewhat different fashion, but as surely, the pivotal battle in the south was the furious fight of Cherubusco. Zachary Taylor had broken the power of Mexico; now to complete the conquest came, with a well-disciplined force of ten thousand Americans — regulars, volunteers and war-ships* — Winfield Scott, the victor of Lundy's Lane, the commander-in-chief of the armies of the United States.

It was the spring of 1847. On the twenty-third of March Vera Cruz, the chief seaport of the Southern Republic, fell before the destructive cannonade of the American batteries. On the eighteenth of April Twiggs' brigade carried by storm the entrenchments on the bristling heights of Cerro Gordo; the men of Shields' and Riley's commands charged the fort and batteries; Santa Anna's fifteen thousand fled for their lives toward the capital, and the famous wooden leg of their artful but intrepid commander was left on the field as a reminder of his hasty flight.

By August the soldiers of Scott had climbed the Sierras from whose crest, as had Cortez and his men three centuries before, they looked down into the lovely Valley of Mexico. From Pueblo to the city of Mexico, the National Road, which was the main approach to the capital, was defended by every device known to a desperate people and an army of over thirty thousand men had rallied to Santa Anna's call to repel the northern invasion.

But, nothing daunted, Scott advanced to Ayatta and looking off at the capital city only fifteen miles distant awaited the report of his engineers. "The Mexicans outnumber us

---

* General Scott's invading force comprised four regiments of artillery, eight of infantry, one of mounted riflemen, and detachments of dragoons — "the then standing army of the United States;" added to these regulars were eight volunteer regiments of infantry and one of cavalry.

four to one," they said. "Yonder fortress of El Penon, between the lakes, commands the road. Its capture will cost you fully a third of your army."

"Is there no other approach to the city?" Scott inquired.

"None but the mule-path around Lake Chalco, to the south, and over the lava beds," was the reply.

"Can we get our cannon and wagons over the mule-path?" the general asked.

"Only by hard work," said the engineers.

"Then make it passable," Scott commanded. "We'll go by the mule-path. The best way to march on an enemy is by the way he least expects you to take."

The road was "fixed"; the detour around the lakes was made; and by the mule-path and over the ragged lava beds Scott's ten thousand eluded the entrenched enemy and approached their capital. The city of Mexico, beautiful for situation, the historic metropolis of Montezuma's fabled kingdom, was, at the time of Scott's advance, inhabited by one hundred and fifty thousand people and defended by thirty-five thousand soldiers.

At the hill of Contreras, in the valley beyond the lava beds, forty-five hundred Americans burst like a storm upon Valencia's seven thousand and in an action of seventeen minutes sent them flying toward Cherubusco with a loss of seven hundred dead, and nine hundred prisoners.

Around the fortified convent of San Pablo de Cherubusco Santa Anna had concentrated an army of thirty thousand men. Scott's available force was scarcely more than eight thousand, but it was a determined and jubilant eight thousand, flushed with victory and confident of success.

The convent-castle bristled with cannon. The Mexican

guns commanded every approach. The Mexican army was in position, determined now to strike one last and overwhelming blow for victory against the northern invaders.

But no such obstacles as fortress, guns or masses of men can stay the march of the Americans. Right on they push. Through the maguey groves, through the cornfields and vegetable gardens, through the ambuscade of dense and overhanging foliage their resistless march goes on. On front and flank they fall remorselessly, while the Third Infantry, with a furious charge, dash at the embattled convent, breached by Taylor's battery, and carry it by storm. Useless to contend against such merciless fighters as these, O, Mexican patriots! Yet fight they do and nobly, though to little purpose. Straight against those wavering ranks ride Kearney's cavalrymen, down upon them charge Shields and Pierce, across the ditches, careless of shot and shell, spring Worth's infantrymen. The Mexicans give way, they turn to flight and streaming along the causeway, "in one wild, panic-stricken mass" they seek the uncertain security of the city's walls while the victorious riders of Harney's cavalry-troop pursue them even to the very gate of their imperiled capital.

On that twentieth of August the fate of Mexico was decided. Ten thousand Mexicans were lost to the Republic as killed, wounded or prisoners; of the Americans, less than a thousand fell. Looked at as a stirring episode of war it was one of the most wonderful and complete victories ever attained on American soil. American pluck and American discipline had overcome unorganized and ill-led bravery in the mass.

Less than a month later, despite the wily ways and desperate treachery of Santa Anna, and after the terrible fights at Molino del Rey, upon the storied hill of Chapultepec and at the gates of the city, the capital fell. Scott's little army of less than seven thousand men marched into the fallen town and Mexico lay at the feet of her conquerors. The war was over.

It was a war brilliant in execution, dramatic in action, marvelous in success. It was the most picturesque contest waged on American soil since the days of the conquistadores; it was crowded with excitement, prolific of peril, tingling with achievement.

Politically the war against Mexico was a grave mistake. Waged for aggrandizement and conquest against a weaker and less intelligent neighbor it was a blot on American justice, a stain on American honor. The new territory that it added to the United States and which might have been peacefully purchased for twenty-five millions of dollars cost the North American Republic one hundred and thirty millions of dollars and twenty thousand lives. Its very success brought about sectionalism and bickering and its final fruits were the war between the States. It was, so far as the American people were concerned, a contest that must ever recall the query of little Peterkin and the reply of old Casper in Southey's well-known ballad:

> "'And everybody praised the Duke
> Who this great fight did win.'
> 'But what good came of it at last?'
> Quoth little Peterkin.
> 'Why, that I cannot tell,' said he,
> 'But 'twas a famous victory.'"

But how few of us regard the utilitarian side of a question when our ears are filled with the sound of martial music, our eyes fixed on the doing of martial deeds. Politically the war against Mexico was a grave mistake; popularly it was a mighty success. Against the greatest odds the ability of the American soldier had been tested and his valor proven to all. It trained the citizen to warfare and afforded a school of instruction from which graduated those whose names in the greater conflict of twenty years after became as household words in the North and South.

"The Mexican war," says Professor Soley, "showed few mistakes, because the officers were well trained, and as a necessary consequence the troops were in a short time well trained also. The War of 1812 on the American side was a war of amateurs; that with Mexico was a war of professional soldiers and strategists."

It was military skill as well as personal valor that forced the fighting at Palo Alto, and held the key to the position at Buena Vista; that made Doniphan's victorious march into Chihuahua — "as arduous and exacting of courage and persistency as Hannibal's crossing the Appenines;" that circumvented a wily foeman by the detour through the lava beds about Lake Chalco and directed the assault up the rocky sides of Chapultepec. The leaders in the Mexican war were indeed no amateurs.

And, despite the grumbling of such suppositious soldiers as Mr. Lowell's "Birdofredum Sawin" there was glory both for general and private from the banks of the Rio Grande and the fortresses of Vera Cruz to the passes of the Sierras and the gates of Mexico. In every battle was the prowess of the American soldier displayed. It was no holiday war — no victory over cowards and cravens. The Americans accomplished a task in their modern conquest of Mexico beset with greater difficulties than was that of Cortez and his companions. The foemen they encountered, so Mr. Ober declares, were "active and intelligent, equally well equipped and versed in the science of war with themselves; the country throughout its length and breadth was alive with hatred of the invaders." Every battle was stubbornly contested. "The Mexicans," says Mr. Ladd, "poured out their blood like water in the defense of their country's honor. But the courage and perseverance of the Americans were more than equal for their desperation and patriotism."

Against Mexican bravery was pitted American valor. In every action the stars and stripes waved above gallant endeavor and dashing deed. Blake's intrepid reconnoissance in face of all the foe at Palo Alto; May's marvelous charge at Resaca de la Palma; the stubborn courage of Doniphan's dauntless Missouri fighters at Sacramento; the exploits of "the Bloody First" at Monterey; O'Brien's plucky stand at Beuna Vista; Harney's fearless climb up the slope of Cerro Gordo; Persifal Smith's gallant capture of the fortified camp of Contreras (considered by General Scott one of the most brilliant feats in all the annals of war); the terrific charge of the Third Infantry at Cherubusco; McIntosh's desperate dash at Molino del Rey; Howard's scaling of the walls of Chapultepec; McKenzie's resistless rush through the San Cosme gate — these are but selected episodes of battle that had their counterparts in every engagement of the war and placed the daring of the American soldier on a par with the generalship and skill of the great leaders in the conflict — Taylor and Kearney, Scott and Worth and those other general officers whose names are inseparably linked with the records of our war against Mexico.

And those who fell! Disease, more dread than lance thrust or saber stroke, than musket wound or crash of booming cannon, cut down five to one of those who fell in battle. There is no poetry in wasted bodies or ruined character; these find no blazoning line on roll of bravery or certificate of honor. Theirs is the record on the dark and repellent side of war. Only the heroic dead are honored.

And above all those who fell in the fury and carnage of this expensive and unnecessary war the noblest monument reared by those who honored them was surely that stirring threnody of their comrade, the soldier-poet, Theodore O'Hara of Kentucky:

> "The muffled drum's sad roll has beat
>   The soldiers' last tattoo!
> No more on life's parade shall meet
>   That brave and fallen few.
> On Fame's eternal camping ground
>   Their silent tents are spread
> And Glory guards with solemn round
>   The Bivouac of the Dead.
>
> "No rumor of the foe's advance
>   Now swells upon the wind;
> No troubled thought at midnight haunts
>   Of loved ones left behind;
> No vision of the morrow's strife
>   The warrior's dream alarms;
> No braying horn, nor screaming fife
>   At dawn shall call to arms.
>
> "The neighboring troop, the flashing blade,
>   The bugle's stirring blast,
> The charge, the dreadful cannonade,
>   The din and shout are past —
> Nor war's wild note, nor glory's peal,
>   Shall thrill with fierce delight
> Those breasts that nevermore may feel
>   The rapture of the fight.
>
> . . . . . .
>
> "Sons of the dark and bloody ground
>   Ye must not slumber there
> Where stranger steps and tongue resound

Along the heedless air,
Your own proud land's heroic soil
  Should be your fitter grave.
She claims from war its richest spoil —
  The ashes of her brave.

. . . . . .

"Rest on, embalmed and sainted dead!
  Dear as the blood ye gave;
No impious footsteps here shall tread
  The herbage of your grave.
Nor shall your glory be forgot
  While Fame her record keeps
Or Honor points the hallowed spot
  Where Valor proudly sleeps."

CHAPTER X.

HORSE, FOOT AND DRAGOON.

THE Mexican War was a practical school of the soldier. Its thorough but rapid turning of recruits into fighters, its forced marches, frequent engagements, hard service and daring deeds — all in a hostile country and against heavy odds — tested the endurance as it tried the courage of men, while the enthusiasm of success strengthened the weak, inspired the timid and gave to every man upon whose pistol belt gleamed the northern eagle, the manner and appearance of the veteran soldier.

The men of Doniphan's command, Missouri volunteers all, who marched two thousand miles overland to the invasion of Chihuahua, saw nine months of hard service before receiving a dollar of pay. But as they stood on Sacramento Hill, twelve hundred and sixty weary men facing five thousand fresh and determined Mexicans, their leader rode from rank to rank. "I could see nothing," he says, "but the stern resolve to conquer or to die. There was no trepidation and no pale faces." Half-rations, hard marches, no clothes and no pay had neither conquered their determination nor dampened their valor. "They curse and praise their country in the same breath," said Colonel Doniphan; "but they fight for her all the time!"

And the undaunted spirit that filled these overworked Missouri volunteers and gave them victory at Brazito, Sacramento, and Chihuahua lived as well in the breasts of all — volunteers and regulars alike — who made up the victorious armies of conquest and occupation in the Mexican War.

To those who imagine that the soldiers of the Mexican War were furnished by the Southern States alone, the figures will tell a different story. Of the hundred thousand fighting men who marched across the Mexican border, twenty-seven thousand were United States regulars; Texas, naturally, as the section directly interested in the conflict, headed the roll of volunteers with eight thousand troops; Louisiana, as the nearest neighbor, came next with nearly eight thousand also; but Illinois and Ohio contributed quite as many men as did Kentucky and Tennessee; New York sent nearly twice as many as did Virginia; Massachusetts and South Carolina furnished an equal number; Pennsylvania sent more than Mississippi; Michigan more than North Carolina; New Jersey more than Florida; Indiana more than Georgia, Maryland and Arkansas combined. Despite the claim that it was "the Southerners' war" it was the Nation's war, in which men of the North and the South marched shoulder to shoulder and fought with equal bravery on bloody fields.

The war was over. The volunteers returned to their homes. The fighting strength of the regulars, grown to over thirty thousand, was reduced to a peace footing of ten thousand. Once again the watchword of the nation was that of the good old Roman emperor: *Æquanimitas*.

If the war against Mexico, among the numerous practical results that it brought about in the more efficient development of the school of the soldier, created a stronger feeling of comradship and union among the officers and men of the regular army than had before existed, it also improved the condition and soldierly standing of the militia engaged therein and sent the volunteers back to their respective States more thoroughly soldiers than they had ever been before.

A marked improvement in the State soldiery was everywhere apparent and the fuss and farce of the old-time drill and muster-days gave place to something like soldierly bearing and real military organization. There was still existing in the tactics that directed the training and evolutions of the regiments much that was cumbersome, old-fashioned and unnecessary. Hardee's Tactics had, indeed, superseded those prepared by General Scott and which were as involved and unwieldy as the flint-lock musket upon the use of which this old-time manual of arms was based. But not all the drilling was done by Hardee's tactics — "which was nothing more," declares General Grant, "than common-sense and the progress of the age applied to Scott's system" — until well on toward the opening of the Civil War. In 1855 Hardee's Tactics were adopted by the Government as the manual for West Point and in the regular army, but in many of the militia regiments the "halt" and "forward march" that preceded and followed every change in the order of march showed that the evolutions of those by-gone days of the flint-lock had not entirely lost their sway.

The military academy at West Point, in the mid-years of the nineteenth century, was increasing in importance and acquiring for itself a wider and more kindly sentiment of popular respect than had been its due in the earlier stage of its existence.

First suggested in 1783 by Colonel Pickering the quartermaster-general of the Revolutionary army, authorized by Congress in 1794 and established in 1802 with forty artillery cadets and ten engineers, it grew but slowly until the War of 1812 proved the incapacity and the lack of training among the officers of the army. From that date the school grew alike in numbers and in efficiency. And yet, despite its real usefulness, this "school for generals" was esteemed by the people at large as little better than an expensive toy that the Government would better do away with. In fact, in December, 1839, a bill was introduced into Congress looking to the abolishment of the military academy. Though this bill never passed the fact of its being introduced is an indication of that popular disapproval of the existence of such a school in a peaceful nation which, in a ruder way, was illustrated by an anecdote that General Grant tells of his early career. Returning after his graduation to his home in Ohio, as big a man, in his own estimation as General Scott, the commander-in-chief himself, and in all the glory of a new uniform his pride experienced a grievous fall through the "humor" of the dissipated stable man of the village tavern. Returning to his home one day young Grant, as he tells us, found this facetious stable-man "parading the streets of Bethel and attending to his duties in the stable, barefooted, but in a pair of sky-blue nankeen pantaloons — just the color of my uniform trousers — with a strip of white cotton sheeting sewed down the outside seams in imitation of mine." It is significant, as indicative of the popular estimation of "West Pointers" at that day that, as General Grant declares, "the joke was a huge one in the minds of many of the people and was much enjoyed by them." This incident of his "salad days" had its effect on all his after life and gave him, he says, a distaste for military uniforms from which he never recovered.

This antagonism to "regular army" ways and methods often displayed itself in times of peace. There was, too, always existing the positive, if unspoken feud born of unnecessary contempt on one side and of equally unnecessary jealousy on the other between the regulars and the militia. Holding the rank of lieutenant in the regular army General Burnside, in 1855, was appointed by the State of Rhode Island major-general of the State militia. In this capacity he once ordered a court-martial for the trial of a commander of a Providence corps. This doughty leader, it seems, had refused to occupy the place in a certain Fourth of July procession to which the General had assigned him, alleging as the reason for his non-appearance that the day was rainy and that he did not wish to damage the new uniforms of his men. But when the court-martial for the trial of this disobedient officer had been ordered the governor of the State, as commander-in-chief, interfered and dissolved the court. General Burnside promptly resigned his commission as major-general of the State militia whereupon the State Legislature as a rebuke to the "arrogance" of a regular army officer elected as his successor the very officer who was to have been tried for disobedience to orders. Far too often have the exigencies and expediences of politics interfered with military discipline and success.

There are always those in every community who, in time of peace are ready to prepare for war. And this is well. Statesmen may see the value and proclaim the necessity of an organized militia. "The United States," wrote Washington in 1793, "ought not to indulge a persuasion that, contrary to the order of human events, they will forever keep at a distance those painful appeals to arms with which the history of every other nation abounds. . . . The devising and establishing of a well-regulated militia would be a genuine source of legislative honor and a perfect title to public gratitude." "As the greatest danger to liberty," said Franklin, "is from large standing armies, it is best to prevent them by an effectual provision for a good militia." "Whenever the militia comes to an end or is despised and neglected," wrote John Adams in 1823, "I shall consider this Union dissolved and the liberties of North America lost forever. National defense is one of the cardinal duties of a statesman."

But statesmen, as a rule, are not the real organizers of the fighting material of a nation. Such work must come from those who represent that outgrowth of the martial spirit that, even among a people absorbed in trade, is ever asserting itself.

The days of peace that intervened between the close of the war with Mexico and the opening of the rebellion exhibited a better conception and a more practical solution of the militia problem than had the earlier years of the century. The old days of the "umbrella and cornstalk militia" of the village muster and carousing "training time" had given place to a better discipline. In certain States the composition and efficiency of the so-styled "crack" regiments gave real importance to the organization of what was known as the National Guard and the country, when its time of stress arrived found itself the possessor of a fair number of trained soldiers whose schooling in arms could be put to practical use and who by their promptness, their zeal and their excellence in discipline really stood in the gap and offered the first successful barrier to armed rebellion. Such regiments, to name certain examples, were the Sixth and Eighth Massachusetts and the Seventh New York.

But, after all, the little regular army of the United States — amounting in 1850 to less than twelve thousand men — was the only actual fighting force that, during the years of peace, upheld the name and kept alive the record of the American Soldier. Commanded by Major-General Winfield Scott, a veteran of three wars, the rank and file of the army — "horse, foot and dragoon" — did much to help in the opening and development of the new lands that, with each new year, were becoming the homes of busy and persistent communities.

Conveying emigrant trains to the widening West, garrisoning the coast-line and the frontier, fighting Indians, escorting exploring expeditions — the life of the American Soldier even in "the piping times of peace," was by no means the profitless and lazy profession that so many pictured it.

The officers were, for the most part, men trained in the military academy of the nation to command and care for those placed under their leadership and charge. They were, as General Marcy assures us, "generally men of intelligence and culture, who entertained the most exalted conceptions of integrity and moral personal responsibility."

That they were brave on occasion the record of many a frontier fight will prove; that they were not lax in discipline the thousand tales of garrison life attest — one post commandant might be mentioned whose police service was so thorough that he has been known, on discovering a quid of tobacco or the stump of a cigar lying in the walks on the parade ground, to call out a police party of several men with hand carts and shovels to remove the obnoxious obstructions; that they were jealous, each, of their own individual arm of the service and had an exalted opinion of their respective duties is shown by the anecdote told of General Bragg of the artillery and a Mexican veteran, who resigned from the army in 1856 because Jefferson Davis, then Secretary of War, ordered him with his battery to the Indian country, as Bragg expressed it, "to chase Indians with six-pounders."

As to the men themselves who filled the ranks of the slender army when on a peace footing it must be admitted that they were of "all sorts and conditions." The regular army was the last resort of those who, unsuccessful or indolent in the field of active labor and of business pursuits, shirked the hot fire of competition before which men must rise or fall by their own exertions and contented themselves with being mere musket-bearers, at the beck and call of their appointed leaders.

Many good men, really fond of the soldiers' life, were to be found in the ranks, but there was both pith as well as reason in the excuse of an old soldier, put on his defense for some breach of garrison discipline, that the court "could scarcely expect to find the entire catalogue of cardinal virtues embodied in every individual specimen of a class of men who only received for their services the paltry compensation of six dollars a month."

It was a "paltry compensation" for what was in the main a dull routine. But dull routine can be hard and tiring work. Listen to this extract from a soldier's diary as, off on New Mexican plains in the year 1854 a tired trumpeter recorded his labors for the day: "February 1st. I commenced the day this morning by being orderly bugler for the commanding officer, and at half-past eight in the morning attended guard-mounting; immediately after, saddled up and rode two miles and assisted at digging a grave; returned at half-past twelve and started again at one with the funeral procession, after which was marched home; dressed for evening parade, marched back again to the corral or stable, assisted in flogging a deserter, came home, ate supper, and here I am, scratching it down in the old journal. Some people surmise that a soldier's life is a lazy one, but soldiers themselves think otherwise."

It was dull routine, but even out of this comes sometimes brilliant flashes of bravery, instances of duty doggedly done yet with a persistence that amounts to heroism. What more dramatic than the equal duel — man to man and gun to gun — of Lieutenant David Bell and White Wolf the Apache chief, each with twenty-three followers? It was during the Indian troubles in New Mexico in the fifties and White Wolf had been guilty of an especially atrocious outrage which Lieutenant Bell burned to avenge. Both parties met on a scout. A parley led only to perplexities and as words were of no avail, lieutenant and chief, dragoon and brave, each picked out an opponent and, man to man, sought to fight it out. With shout and war-whoop, with cavalry charge and erratic Indian dash, all the time giving shot for shot was this duel by wholesale fought out; twenty-one of the forty-six combatants were killed or wounded; scarcely a man on either side was without hurt of some sort. At last White Wolf fell; the remnant of his band fled and the duel was ended.

So, too, Lieutenant Hood with but seventeen men, ambushed by over fifty Lipan and Comanche warriors, in those same risky days on the plains, showed both pluck and endurance that were heroic in the extreme. Outnumbered, three to one, he yet encouraged his men to fight for their lives. Again and again, with ringing cheers the brave seventeen charged the yelling savages and mingled in a hand-to-hand conflict. The odds were against the seventeen. Six had already fallen beneath the

MARCY'S PERILOUS MARCH.

Indian fire. Hood's saber arm hung useless at his side, back and still backward were they pressed, their rifles empty, their strength almost spent. "Out with your revolvers, boys," shouted Hood, courageous to the last; "one more shot; we mustn't give it up!" Inspired by his superb courage the little command turned on the enemy in a fierce revolver charge. It was the desperate last chance and so impetuous was it that the Indians fell back, turned and fled. Then with empty revolvers the troopers, leaving twenty-two of their antagonists dead or dying galloped from the field that had well-nigh been their grave, victors over an ambuscade that it seemed impossible to break.

As plucky, too, though in endurance rather than in desperate fight, were the men of Marcy's command who, in November, 1857, went westward from Fort Bridger on an expedition for exploration and relief. Through an almost trackless wilderness, across lofty and rugged mountains they struggled on in the very depth of winter loyal to their duty and striving for results that to them personally could be of but little value or advantage. The snows grew deeper and deeper; the cold became more and more intense; their horses and pack-animals starved and fell by the way; supplies gave out; the suffering grew almost unbearable and yet not a man murmured or complained. They had volunteered for this desperate service and they would keep their promise or die. For fifty-one days the weary march continued. The path through the snow could only be made to bear weight by the efforts of the advance men of the party who on hands and knees pressed and hardened the treacherous and impalpable mass. For the last twelve days of the march the only food was the tough "mule-steak" cut from the starved beasts of burden and sprinkled with gunpowder in lieu of salt and pepper. "I am indebted," wrote General Marcy, years after, "for my existence at this moment to the unparalleled fortitude, endurance and sufferings of a noble little band of soldiers who nearly sacrificed their own lives to extricate me from the perils of a winter's journey over the snow-clad summits of the Rocky Mountains."

Almost as full of hardships and quite as eloquent in determination, pluck and a dogged perseverance, was Colonel Washington's march to Sante Fé in 1849, in which Lieutenant Stein and his company of the Second Dragoons fought against Indians, thirst and hunger on New Mexican deserts and "brave and vigilant, never murmured, but showed the noblest traits of men and soldiers." The private's weary march and patient round of duty has often contained more of romance and displayed more of real valor than all the momentary excitement of the headlong charge or the fiery crash of battle.

However hard was the private soldier's life that of the officer whom he was bound to obey was scarcely easier because of rank or station. General Albert Sidney Johnston, paymaster of the army from 1849 to 1854, made six annual tours of the Texas frontier traveling each year, in rough country riding, over four thousand miles. Lieutenant William P. Sanders, in pursuit of deserters, in 1857, accompanied by but one man, rode from Fort Crittenden, Utah, to Los Angeles, California, over a rugged and dangerous road, captured and delivered up the deserters and returned to Fort Crittenden, a journey of sixteen hundred miles, in less than sixty days. Lieutenant A. E. Burnside in 1857 rode with special dispatches twelve hundred miles from El Paso to Washington, facing and escaping all sorts of dangers and reaching Washington fully a month before the civilian who was his rival in the race.

A soldier's first duty is obedience. The "thinking bayonet" which was a popular characterization of the intelligent soldier during the Great Rebellion has really no place in the ranks of those enlisted men known as the regular army — musket bearers, who must know no duty but unquestioning obedience. Whether the authority in power ordered troops to put down threatened insurrection in South Carolina in 1832, or to guard in Boston streets a fugitive slave sent back to his owners by due process of law in 1854 the soldiers who, north or south, east or west, marched in the ranks of the regulars had no business to question the orders of their superiors:

> "Theirs not to reason why,
> Theirs but to do or die."

It is this blindness to everything but duty, this readiness to obey orders lead where they may, that gives to the "regulars" a certain assurance and stamp of real authority that neither volunteer nor militia-man can possess save by long service and experience. The "regulars" are the representatives of Government and the Law. Their measured tread and machine-like discipline are able to stay every wave of opposition, every advance of warring factions and of unlawful organization. The majesty of authority that attached to the legionaries of old Rome has been the attribute of every regular army from ancient times even to the present day.

This, so far as the United States Army is concerned, was especially noticeable in the unhappy days of the Kansas troubles of 1856, when the new State, torn by civil feud and rent by the strife for possession waged by " Free Soilers " and " Pro-Slavery men," became the scene of disorder, of outrage and of blood. The appearance of the United States Regulars dispatched to the disturbed sections could always stay the fratricidal strife and establish law and order where none before existed. General Cooke in his reminiscences of army life at that time says: "It was part of the education of both parties that they still respected national authority. There was but one flag yet. At Lecompton I rode alone — leaving my forces far behind — in front of an army of thousands, who with cannon-matches lighted, were about to attack that territorial capitol, and ordered them to retire, and the nation's representative was obeyed. The Second Dragoons were prominent in these important services, but with them were the First Cavalry, the Sixth Infantry and a battery of the Fourth Artillery. This force was afterward interposed between a regularly organized army of twenty-seven hundred men and the town of Lawrence which they had marched to attack."

The time came when rebellion rose above authority, and neither regular army nor national government had power to stay the tide of civil war. But when that day came many of those whose position gave strength and form to the army of the United States themselves deserted their post and were false to their oaths of allegiance. And when leaders fall away how can the army maintain itself intact? It is said that General Sherman, who, when the rebellion broke out, was the superintendent of the Louisiana Military Academy recognized months afterwards in the prisoners taken in war most of the cadets of his institution who when the conflict came hastened to enlist in the Confederate army. So, too, West Point men and brother officers of the regular army found themselves divided by questions of duty and of loyalty and met as enemies on bloody fields in the stubborn battles of the Civil War.

For that desperate hour, indeed, officers and men through

all the years that intervened between the Mexican War and the attack on Sumter were all unconsciously preparing. The military incidents of these days of peace were but few and far between, but the efficiency and discipline that were displayed by the small standing army of the United States (never in all those years exceeding twelve thousand men), by certain of the militia regiments of the National Guard and by such superbly-drilled private organizations as Ellsworth's Zouaves all bore fruit when the call to arms rang out in the opening days of the Great Rebellion.

There were certain uneasy Americans who were anxious for excitement or ambitious for gain and so made haste to join themselves to the filibustering expeditions of Lopez the Spaniard and of William Walker the American (that "gray-eyed man of destiny" who fell a victim to his own unlawful schemes). They all met at last with defeat, but even in this lawless adventuring they were but schooling themselves for the days of real war that were coming on apace. The militia-men who responded to the call to put down riot in New York City in 1849 and in Kansas in 1856 were quick to respond to the call for more serious duty when the iron hail rattled against the walls of Sumter.

And on Western plains the brave regulars who penetrated untrodden wildernesses and braved hunger and thirst, weariness and cold for the punishment of restless Indians or the extension of the governmental authority acquired a steadiness and a nerve that were to serve them well when the War Department at last ordered them to act as the nucleus of the nation's defenders in a war that was to lift the American soldier, North, as well as South, to the foremost position among the fighting-men of the world.

"Horse, foot and dragoon" alike were being schooled for

greater and more serious service. The dull routine of camp life and of garrison duty, the countless ways in which officers and men sought to relieve the tedium of monotony and manufacture excitement out of unpromising surroundings were soon to be exchanged for active service and stirring times. But of these neither militia-man nor regular yet dreamed. The one like the sober business man he was, stood behind his counter or sat at his desk thinking more of dollars than of rifle and saber; the other in sea-coast garrison or in frontier post lived careless of the future, weary only of the present; or perhaps, off on a scout in the far Indian country he slept serenely with his holsters as his pillow and the sky as his tent cover, ready to spring to arms when the summons came. With pride in his horse, his uniform and his accoutrements he could sing with ringing and sturdy notes this song of "The Light Dragoons," written by one of his comrades : *

"Good cheer, my steed!
Let thy headlong speed
Dash the dew from the prairie grass.
Shrink not, in the track,
Let the hills fall back
As the ranks of our squadron pass.

"At the fall of night,
In the gray twilight,
When I've combed thy tangled mane,
'Neath the light of the moon
Then the light dragoon
Will lie down by his steed again.

"When sleep is done,
And the rising sun
Shall have burnished thy glossy hair,

* Lieutenant E. P. Davidson, an officer of the First U. S. Dragoons.

> To horse again
> And we'll scour the plain
> And beat up the red-man's lair."

And after each verse, with a boisterous energy that would set the echoes ringing through all those western hills, his comrades would roll out the chorus :

> Then up, my steed!
> The wind's wild speed
> Is but slow to thy headlong flight ;
> And we'll rein up soon,
> And the light dragoon
> With his charger shall sleep tonight.

CHAPTER XI.

BOYS OF 'SIXTY-ONE.

T O the States arrayed against the national authority, the greatest of American presidents said in his first inaugural, "in your hands, my dissatisfied fellow-countrymen, and not in mine is the momentous issue of civil war. The Government will not assail you. You can have no conflict without being yourselves the aggressors."

All too soon did Abraham Lincoln receive the answer to his message of kindly forbearance. And when, at half-past four o'clock on that dark and raw April morning in 1861 that answer came in the shot that went hurtling over the water toward the dimly-outlined ramparts of beleagured Sumter all men knew its import. Civil war had begun.

The result of that bombardment of a national fortress by the nation's recreant sons proved vastly different from the popular prophecies. There was but one uprising in the North, but one in the South. The armed protests against war which, so it was conjectured, would be made both North and South failed to materialize. There was no attempt at coercion in favor of union in the South, none in favor of secession in the North. "The Union forever!" and "Hurrah for Liberty!" were the only shouts that rallied young patriots in the North and young rebels in the South around the tables of the recruiting sergeants.

Enthusiasm is contagious. Of it great enterprises are born, from it great achievements gain their noblest impulses. But unorganized enthusiasm is of no lasting value; men must be molded as well as inspired if results are to be attained.

When, the day after Sumter, President Lincoln's call for seventy-five thousand volunteers came as an appeal for instant succor, twice that number of Northern men clamored to be led against the nation's foes. In response to the call for fifty thousand troops to make good the assertions of the new "Confederacy" over three hundred thousand men were offered by the South. Sixteen Northern States and seven Southern ones in that historic spring of 1861 stood facing each other in the attitude of war. But neither the North nor the South was prepared for the conflict. Arms and appointments were lacking. The recruits who were accepted were raw, undisciplined and inexperienced. In the first great clash of arms at Bull Run the forces of disorganization met and men awoke to the knowledge, dearly bought, of how valueless for real results is enthusiasm alone. Defeated in that bloody encounter the North was still the greater gainer, for Bull Run was a deeper disaster to the Confederate than to the Union forces. By it, the latter were stiffened into determined action, the former, lulled by false hopes, relaxed the vigor their desperate fortunes needed.

Brought face to face with stern and sudden need the nation learned its own incompetency. The slender regular army, upon which it should have relied until its reserve fighting force could be gathered for the master-stroke, was scattered far and wide, deliberately dismembered by the shrewd treachery of the traitorous war-secretary Floyd. On the fifth of April, 1861, less than four hundred out of the seventeen thousand troops who constituted the regular army were available for the defense of Washington. The rest were distributed throughout the entire country with but imperfect facilities to bring them to the threatened Capitol. This distribution, according to General Scott's detailed report, was as follows: Department of the East, 3894; Department of the West, 3584; Department of Texas, 2258; Department of New Mexico, 2624; Department of Utah, 685; Department of the Pacific, 3382; miscellaneous, 686; grand total, officers and men, 17,113.

And upon these, even if available, who could rely? It was a time for breaking faith. Men, educated at Government expense, were proving recreant to their oaths of fealty and deserting the flag they had sworn to defend. Twiggs, a veteran fighter of the Mexican War, treacherously surrendered his entire command, the Department of Texas (nineteen army posts in all together with twelve hundred thousand dollars worth of military property), to the authorities of that far-off State. Even the sole safeguard of the imperilled nation seemed slipping away.

And yet there was loyalty in the regular army worthy of eternal remembrance. The ranks were faithful though their leaders might prove false. It is asserted that there were, in 1861, military posts abandoned by all the commissioned officers, of which not one of the enlisted men proved untrue.

The regulars surrendered by Twiggs in Texas, threatened to kill any man who attempted to disarm them and marched away with the stained and bullet-torn old flag of the Eighth

GOOD-BY.

Regiment streaming above them while their band played national airs.

And against the hesitating disloyalty of such notable leaders as Lee and the two Johnstons there shone brightly out the unwavering fidelity of others, also Southern born, to whom loyalty to the old flag and fealty to their plighted word were paramount to the fictitious claims of any rebellious State. "I am a Southern man," said Major Robert Anderson, the hero of Sumter, "but I have been assigned to the defense of Charleston Harbor, and I intend to defend it." And Winfield Scott, the general of the army, the veteran of many a fight, when urged to "follow his State" unhesitatingly declared: "Such a proposal is a mortal insult. I have served my country under the flag of the Union for more than fifty years, and as long as God permits me to live I will defend that flag with my sword, even if my own native State assails it."

But if the regulars could not be made at once available their place was made good by those next to them in efficiency and discipline. The uniformed militia were quick to respond. Within forty-eight hours after the President had issued his call for troops the Sixth Regiment of Massachusetts was on its way to Washington, and, before another forty-eight hours had passed, had dyed the stones of Baltimore with the first blood of the civil war.

Hard behind them pressed the New York Seventh and the Massachusetts Eighth. Other regiments followed fast. The beleaguered capital was saved. So surely can discipline conquer doubt. For it is said that as the New York Seventh marched up Pennsylvania Avenue on their way to the White House, "with their well-formed ranks, their exact military step, their soldierly bearing, their gayly floating flags, and the inspiring music of their splendid regimental band, they seemed to sweep all thought of danger and all taint of treason not only out of that great national thoroughfare, but out of every human heart in the Federal city. The presence of this single regiment seemed to turn the scales of fate. Cheer upon cheer greeted them, windows were thrown up, houses opened, the population came forth upon the streets as for a holiday. It was an epoch in American history. For the first time, the combined spirit and power of Liberty entered the nation's capital." *

Recruiting went on rapidly. New regiments were commissioned with marvelous speed. Volunteers poured into Washington at the rate of four thousand a day. The whole loyal North was on fire. Such incidents as the first shot against Sumter, the attack on the Massachusetts Sixth in Baltimore, and the famous order of General Dix: " If any man attempt to haul down the American flag shoot him on the spot!" were the strongest incentives to patriotism. In teeming city, and bustling village, in gossipy cross-road store and in the quiet farmhouse on western prairie and eastern hillside, the stout young fellows who were not carried away with the hurrah of enthusiasm felt keenly, as one private expressed it, that he should have to go at last or forfeit his birthright as an American citizen. War was in the air. The labors of peaceful life were neglected. The citizen-soldier was awaking to a sense of his duty.

A city of tents sprang up along the Potomac. Soldiers were everywhere. They came from every Northern State, their speech "bewraying" them, as it did the men of Galilee. Yankee and Hoosier, Knickerbocker and Buckeye, Green Mountain boy and men of the prairies and the lakes they were comrades in camp, brothers in effort and duty. They were of all stages of greenness and all grades of efficiency from the raw recruit who scarcely knew the "right face!" from the "shoulder

---

* Nicolay & Hay: " Abraham Lincoln, A History."

arms!" and the equally fresh captain who would command his company to "Gee around that hole!" to the crack militia-man or the veteran Indian fighter, the West Point graduate and the dignified general of division.

Eternal drilling is the price of discipline. It must come before advance or victory but it is tedious work to the enthusiastic soldier whose one desire is a chance to display his valor. "There are some things," says Private Goss remembering those first days of preparation, "that take down even excess of patriotism. The musket after an hour's drill seemed heavier and less ornamental than it had looked to be. It takes a raw recruit some time to learn that he is not to think or suggest, but obey. Some never do learn. I doubt if my patriotism during my first three weeks' drill was quite knee-high."

But true patriotism outlives the drudgery of drill even as it burns high and clear before the supreme act of enlistment. And how high and clear that flame did burn, the silent records of many a Northern home could well attest. The young blood of the nation was surging toward the field of action, too hot to be cooled by thought of drudgery, too rapid to be stayed by plea or threat or any home restriction. The opening months of that first war summer, when men were seeking the recruiting office or steadily pressing southward were among the most dramatic phases of the nation's stirring story. One of the noblest of the many noble war poems* has grandly caught and kept the inspiration:

> "The drum's wild roll awakes the land, the fife is calling shrill;
> Ten thousand starry banners blaze on town and bay and hill;
> Our crowded streets are throbbing with the soldiers' measured tramp;
> Among our bladed cornfields gleam the white tents of the camp.

* A poem by Ellery Channing read before the Phi Beta Kappa Society of Harvard College in 1861.

The thunders of the rising war hush Labor's drowsy hum,
And heavy to the ground the first dark drops of battle come;
The souls of men flame up anew, the narrow heart expands,
And woman brings her patient faith to nerve her eager hands.
Thank God! we are not buried yet, though long in trance we lay —
Thank God! the fathers need not blush to own their sons to-day!

"Oh! sad and slow the weeks went by — each held his anxious breath,
Like one who waits in helpless fear some sorrow great as death.
Oh! scarcely was there faith in God, nor any trust in man,
While fast along the southern sky the blighting shadow ran.
It veiled the stars one after one, it hushed the patriot's song,
And stole from men the sacred sense that parteth right and wrong;
Then a red flash, like lightning, across the darkness broke,
And, with a voice that shook the land, the guns of Sumter spoke:
Wake, sons of heroes, wake! the age of heroes dawns again,
Truth takes in hand her ancient sword and calls her loyal men,
Lo, brightly o'er the breaking day shines Freedom's holy star!
Peace cannot cure the sickly time — all hail the healer, War!

"That call was heard by Plymouth Rock, 'twas heard in Boston Bay;
Then up the piney streams of Maine sped on its ringing way,
New Hampshire's rocks, Vermont's green hills, it kindled into flame,
Rhode Island felt her mighty soul bursting her little frame.
The Empire City started up, her golden fetters rent,
And meteor-like across the North the fiery message sent,
Over the breezy prairie lands by bluff and lake it ran,
Till Kansas bent his arm, and laughed to find himself a man.
Then on by cabin and by camp, by stony wastes and sands,
It rang exultant down the sea, where the golden city stands.

" And wheresoe'er the summons came there rose an angry din,
As when upon a rocky coast a stormy tide comes in.
Straightway the fathers gathered voice, straightway the sons arose,
With flushing cheek, as when the East with day's red current glows.
Hurrah! the long despair is past, our fading hopes renew,
The fog is lifting from the land, and lo, the ancient blue!
We learn the secrets of the deeds the sires have handed down,
To fire the youthful soldier's zeal and tend his green renown.
Who lives for country, though his arm feels all her forces flow,
'Tis easy to be brave for truth as for the rose to blow.

"O Law, fair form of Liberty, God's light is on thy brow,
O Liberty, thou soul of Law, God's very self art thou!
One, the clear river's sparkling flood, that clothes the bank with green,
And one, the line of stubborn rock that holds the water in;
Friends whom we cannot think apart, seeming each other's foe,
Twin flowers upon a single stalk, with equal grace that grow;
O, fair ideas! we write your names across our banner's fold,
For you the sluggard's brain is fire, for you the coward bold;
O, daughter of the bleeding past! O, hope the prophets saw!
God give us Law in Liberty, and Liberty in Law!

" Full many a heart is aching with mingled joy and pain,
For those who go so proudly forth and may not come again;
And many a heart is aching for them it leaves behind,
As a thousand tender histories throng in upon the mind.
The old men bless the young men, and praise their bearing high,
The women in the doorways stand to wave them bravely by:
One threw her arms about her boy and said, 'Good-by, my son.
God help thee do the valiant deeds thy father would have done!'
One held up to a bearded man a little child to kiss,
And said, 'I shall not be alone, for thy dear love and this.'
And one, a rosebud in her hand, leant at a soldier's side,
'Thy country needs thee first,' she said, 'be I thy second bride!'

"O, mothers, when around your hearths ye count your cherished ones,
And miss from the enchanted ring the flower of all your sons;
O, wives, when o'er the cradled child ye bend at evening's fall,
And voices which the heart can hear across the distance call;
O, maids, when in the sleepless nights ye ope' the little case
And look till ye can look no more upon the proud young face,
Not only pray the Lord of Life who measures mortal breath,
To bring the absent back unscathed out of the fire of death;
O, pray with that divine content which God's best favor draws,
That whosoever lives or dies He save His holy cause.

" So out of shop and farmhouse, from shore and inland glen,
Thick as the bees in clover time are swarming armed men;
Along the dusty roads in haste the eager columns come,
With flash of sword and muskets' gleam, the bugle and the drum;
Ho! comrades, see the starry flag broad waving at our head.
Ho! comrades, mark the tender light on the dear emblems spread!

OUR BROTHER THE ENEMY.

Our fathers' blood has hallowed it, 'tis part of their renown,
And palsied be the caitiff hand would pluck its glories down;
Hurrah! hurrah! it is our home where'er thy colors fly,
We win with thee the victory, or in thy shadow die:

"O, women, drive the rattling loom, and gather in the hay,
For all the youth, worth love and truth, are marshaled for the fray;
Southward the hosts are hurrying, with banners wide unfurled,
From where the stately Hudson floats the wealth of half the world;
From where amid his clustered isles Lake Huron's waters gleam,
From where the Mississippi pours an unpolluted stream:
From where Kentucky's fields of corn bend in the southern air,
From broad Ohio's luscious vines, from Jersey's orchards fair;
From where, between his fertile slopes, Nebraska's rivers run,
From Pennsylvania's iron hills, from woody Oregon;
And Massachusetts led the van, as in the days of yore,
And gave her reddest blood to cleanse the stones of Baltimore.

"O, mothers, sisters, daughters, spare the tears ye fain would shed,
Who seem to die in such a cause, ye cannot call them dead;
They live upon the lips of men, in picture, bust and song,
And Nature folds them in her heart, and keeps them safe from wrong.
O, length of days is not a boon the brave man prayeth for,
There are a thousand evils worse than death or any war,
Oppression with his iron strength fed on the souls of men,
And License with the hungry brood that haunt his ghastly den;
But like bright stars ye fill the eye, adoring hearts ye draw,
O sacred grace of Liberty! O majesty of Law!

"Hurrah! the drums are beating, the fife is calling shrill,
Ten thousand starry banners flame on town, and bay, and hill;
The thunders of the rising war drown Labor's peaceful hum,
Thank God that we have lived to see the saffron morning come.
The morning of the battle-call, to every soldier dear,
O joy! the cry is "Forward!" O joy! the foe is near!
For all the crafty men of peace have failed to purge the land,
Hurrah! the ranks of battle close, God takes his cause in hand.'

Who, now living, that remembers those stirring days of 'sixty-one would forego the recollection? It was a time of intense excitement, North and South alike — of flag-raising in every town and debate and decision in every home; of eloquent appeals to patriotism in pulpit and on stump; of drilling on every village common; of tenders of troops from every State capital; of warlike preparations in every city; of hurried orders for war material in workshop and foundry; of daily parades; of flag-presentations; of soul-stirring songs and ringing cheers at every patriotic utterance; of quick action; of tearful partings; of hurried good-byes; of tear-wrung God bless yous; of neglected private business; of eternally rolling drums and endlessly marching regiments; of lint-scraping and bandage-tearing; of excitement, enthusiasm and stern determination everywhere. Drake DeKay, a fervid and practical young patriot, stirred by the President's call, closed his shipping office in New York with no more ceremony than to pin this notice on his door: "Gone to Washington. Back at close of war." The youth of the South frenzied with an even intenser excitement clamored to be led against "the mud-sills of the North." The land was mad for war, crazed with enthusiasm, and men on either side the line marked by the doubtful border States, felt each that they alone were right and echoed the poet's cry:

"For all the crafty men of peace have failed to purge the land,
Hurrah! the ranks of battle close; God takes his cause in hand."

There were many impatient souls that as the spring grew to summer felt that Providence "took his cause in hand" all too slowly, there were many trusting hearts that could not fathom why action did not follow enthusiasm and push the war to an instant conclusion. The murder of the gallant Ellsworth, the heroic death at Big Bethel of Greble the young West Pointer and of Winthrop, the brilliant writer, were not, it seemed, quickly avenged. And so out of impatience and desire came the mad demand of those who waited and watched at home: "On to Richmond!" Americans are always prone to rebel at the old adage that bids us "make haste slowly." President and cabinet, military leaders and advisers yielded to the unwise demand of the people. Bull Run was fought against the better judgment of those who should have delayed the hostile meeting — it was fought and the North, in bitter humiliation, saw its legions streaming back to the capital, routed and panic-stricken.

Said General Scott, worn out with worry and the criticism that follows failure: "I am the greatest coward in America, sir. I will prove it. I have fought this battle against my judgment; I think the President of the United States ought to remove me today for doing it. As God is my judge, after my superiors had determined to fight it I did all in my power to make the army efficient. I deserve removal because I did not stand up, when my army was not in a condition for fighting, and resist it to the last."

Bull Run tried the temper as it strengthened the will of the North; it exaggerated the valor as it disorganized the caution of the South. "Brethren, we'd better adjourn this camp-meeting and go home and drill," cried an Illinois minister as the news of the defeat interrupted his sermon. "A few more Bull Run thrashings will bring the Yankees once more under the yoke as docile as the most loyal of our Ethiopian chattels," announced a Southern newspaper.

Really a rout for both sides this first pitched battle of the war was an acknowledged defeat only for those whose legs were longest. Jefferson Davis, seeing the streams of Confederate fugitives pouring from the field considered the day lost. "Battles are not won," said he, "where two or three unhurt men are seen leading away one that is wounded." Private John Tinkham of a Northern regiment declared that after getting the order to retreat he should not have stopped running short of Boston if he had not been halted by a soldier with a musket on the Washington end of Long Bridge.

IN THE RECRUITING OFFICE.

Checked enthusiasm either dies out altogether or is changed into a glorious, because stern and unyielding determination. Out of the gloom of Bull Run sprang such a determination on the part of the North. Its patriotism was too sincere to be wrecked by one set back, its purpose too deep to yield to the appeals of timidity or the arrogance of successful rebellion.* The people, united in a resolution that was only strengthened by disaster, ground their set teeth and bent to their task. Fresh troops were enlisted, new regiments were hastened to the front. Three hundred regiments of fully a thousand men each were dispatched to what were esteemed the places in immediate danger. The statistical record of men present for duty shows that on the first of January, 1862, there were five hundred and twenty-seven thousand two hundred and four Union soldiers in the volunteer army of the United States as against one hundred and fifty-seven thousand on July first.

Of this total nearly two hundred thousand men were upon the muster-rolls of the Army of the Potomac. The disaster at Bull Run had there led to instant change. Worn out by age and infirmities General Scott had resigned and General George B. McClellan, whose brilliant achievements among the hills of Western Virginia had made him a popular hero, was given the command of the Army of the Potomac. At once he proceeded upon his herculean task of organization and discipline.

East and west the forces of union and disunion held back from immediate conflict, striving, instead, to complete the organization so necessary to successful action. The border line was seamed with earthworks, the blockaded coasts bristled with fortifications. The hostile armies faced each other, glaring across a death line that reached from the Atlantic to the mountains of New Mexico — a battle front of fully two thousand miles. This was practically divided into three sections. In the East, McClellan with the Army of the Potomac was opposed to Lee and Johnston with the Army of Northern Virginia; in the

---

* "Had Johnston or Beauregard pushed their success and occupied Washington," says General Sherman, "it would not have changed the result, because twenty millions of free men would never have submitted tamely to the domination of the slaveholder faction."

center Buell with the Army of the Ohio had for his antagonist Albert Sidney Johnston with the Army of the Cumberland; in the west Halleck with the Army of the Missouri was confronted by McCulloch and the Army of the Mississippi.

At last, though all too slowly to suit the impatient North, the tug of war came. It came with varying results and with uncertain efforts, each side as yet feeling its way. Of the half-dozen engagements that took place between the disastrous July of 1861 and the opening months of 1862 scarce one was decisive or really important until the fall of Fort Donelson on the sixteenth of February drew all eyes to the operations in the west that culminated in the famous two days' fight at Shiloh — the first great battle of the Civil War.

So, after all, it was from the west that the first note of victory, the first prophecy of final triumph came. In the east, McClellan now raised to the command of all the armies of the United States, was displaying his wonderful ability as the best organizer of armed troops known to American history; but so jealous was he of his own forces, so desirous of putting every available man into the Army of the Potomac, that he had but scant sympathy for the other divisions of the great army of which he was commanding general. " Every man sent to any other department," says a recent authority, " he regarded as a sort of robbery of the Army of the Potomac." Day after day the same report went to the North : " All quiet on the Potomac ;" day after day president and people grew more anxious, more critical, more impatient.

Who then can wonder that the news from the west sent a thrill of joy through the waiting, weary heart of the north. Grant's stern reply to Buckner, the commander at Fort Donelson: " No terms except an unconditional and immediate surrender can be accepted. I propose to move immediately upon your works," was the answer to the nation's prayer for prompt action and immediate results. They came speedily. Donelson and its fifteen thousand men surrendered to the Union arms. Grant was made a major-general of volunteers. His name was upon every lip. And then came Shiloh.

In the country round about that little log church in Southwestern Tennessee that gave its name to what has been called "the most famous and to both sides the most interesting of the battles of the war," for two long days the bloody conflict raged. Furious, deadly and stubbornly contested this bloodiest battle ever fought west of the Alleghanies gave the key-note to all the succeeding contests of the war — it was fighting to kill because it was fighting to conquer. Forty thousand Northern troops joined battle with an equal number of Southern soldiers. It was a duel to the death. "The troops on both sides," says General Grant, "were American and, united, they need not fear any foreign foe." Divided, alas, their obstinate fight was terrible in its intensity, terrible in its results. Every inch of ground was disputed stubbornly, every possible device for wresting victory from defeat was made use of by both parties. And when after a two days' fight the Southern army turned in flight, its leader dead, its object defeated, its high hopes dashed to earth the loss entailed by that terrible struggle was as appalling as the victory was complete. At least eleven thousand men was the roll in killed and wounded on either side. "If we should read." says Mr. Johnson. "that by some disaster every man. woman and child in the city of Concord, New Hampshire. had been either killed or wounded, and in the next day's paper that the same thing had happened in Montgomery,

Alabama, the loss in life and limb would only equal what took place on the mournful field of Shiloh."

It was a test battle. For the first time Southern dash and discipline had grappled with Northern endurance and discipline, on equal terms and on a fair field. It was the first real battle of the war. For this the Boys of 'Sixty-one had drudged and drilled, for this North and South had been clamorously calling. After Shiloh the Southern boast that a Southern gentleman could whip five Yankees was no more heard; the Northern bravado that the war could not outlast one fair battle died away forever. Both sides now understood that war meant work and that it meant a stubborn death-grapple ere the end could come. Every man who outlived the heated fire of "the hornet's nest" at Shiloh came from the conflict with a higher regard of the fighting qualities of "his brother the enemy" than he had held before.

But though, before Shiloh, no real battle had been fought, the dozen or more engagements had shown the temper of the men who had sprung to arms. Ellsworth at Alexandria and Baker at Ball's Bluff had shown how daring and foolhardiness may run side by side. Lyon the gallant Westerner, shot down while heading a charge at Wilson's Creek — "the bloodiest battle, up to that date, ever fought on American soil" — showed how deep was his patriotism, how determined his purpose by leaving, by his will, his entire fortune to the United States for use in defense of the imperilled nation; Mulligan, holding with but twenty-eight hundred men his post at Lexington, Missouri, against an overwhelming force of fourteen thousand did but prophesy by his bravery his still greater valor which on a later day, at Winchester fight, caused him to say to those who bore him dying, from the field, "Lay me down and save the flag;"

Smith, of the regulars, a loyal "West Pointer," could answer the insinuations that hinted at his disloyalty as he listened with flashing eyes: "Oh! never mind; they'll take it back after my first battle." And "they" did. And this same magnetic leader showed the stuff of which brave men are made when leading a charge at Fort Donelson, cap twirling on sword-point, he shouted: "No flinching now, my lads. Here — this is the way; come on!" and so dashed through to victory.

FOR THE SOLDIERS.

For a while the exuberant spirits of those first volunteers who rushed to the war as to some prolonged picnic lost alike their elasticity and their enthusiasm even, under the routine of the camp and the depressing effect of their surroundings. The men who had gone to the front, swarming over the roofs of freight cars or clinging to the breezy "cow-catcher," who had scaled the walls of the Capitol and frisked like monkeys along its high-hung cornices and water-tables, who had rushed into the water with drawn knives to "tackle" the voracious and deadly sharks and worried the souls of slow-witted "contrabands" by their gibes and pranks — these found discipline a hard word to construe and duty but too often drudgery and weariness. "Mud," says Private Goss, "took the military valor all out of a man. Any one would think from reading the Northern papers that we had macadamized roads over which to charge at the enemy. It would have pleased us much to have seen these 'on to Richmond' people put over a five-mile course in the Virginia mud, loaded with a forty-pound knapsack, sixty rounds of cartridges and haversacks filled with four days' rations."

"The Confederate army," says General Beauregard, "was filled with generous youth who had answered the first call to arms. For certain kinds of field work they were not yet adapted, many of them having come with their baggage and servants. These they had to dispense with, but not to offend their susceptibilities I exacted the least work from them apart from military drills even to the prejudice of important field work when I could not get sufficient negro labor. They 'had come to fight and not to handle the pick and shovel,' they declared emphatically."

It was hard too for recruits to learn that there is really no place in the ranks for the "thinking bayonet"—as some unmilitary folk liked to call the volunteer of '61. "I thought, sir—" a certain private began, but was speedily interrupted. "Think! think!" roared the colonel; "what right have you to think? I do the thinking for this regiment. Go to your quarters!" The rank and file and under officers of a regiment are not taken into the confidence of their superiors. Their duty is simply to obey orders.

And gradually they learned to obey. As the days rolled by and none knew how soon the test of battle might come, discipline came to the aid of duty and made of the raw recruits soldierly fellows, anxious to make proof of their training and show their valor in the face of the foe. "Every army has its driftwood soldiers," says Mr. Coffin, "valiant at the mess table, brave in the story about the bivouac fire, but faint of heart when the battle begins." That this is but too true every battle shows. Bull Run was its earliest proof and even at Shiloh the ten thousand National and Confederate deserters showed the yet uncertain *morale* of the armies — but these recreants are the exception, the minority when the bugle sounds "fall in" and the stirring command to charge means desperate work at hand.

In all those early months of tedious preparation for the greater conflict to which Shiloh was the prelude the soldiers North and South were learning the hard lesson of how to obey. The unwritten romance of the camps could tell of many a fight with pride and many a conquest over self in the hard school of the daily drill and of the lonely picket-line. There is often more of heroism in this latter dangerous duty than on the noisier line of battle and in the daylight charge to death. The silent hero is often the most valorous. The pathetic poem of disputed authorship, so popular during the war, told all too vividly the story of the lonely picket:

> "All quiet along the Potomac," they say,
> "Except now and then a stray picket
> Is shot, as he walks on his beat to and fro,
> By a rifleman hid in the thicket;
> 'Tis nothing — a private or two now and then
> Will not count in the news of the battle;
> Not an officer lost — only one of the men,
> Moaning out, all alone, his death-rattle."
>
> "There's only the sound of the lone sentry's tread,
> As he tramps from the rock to the fountain,
> And he thinks of the two in the low trundle-bed
> Far away in the cot on the mountain.
> His musket falls slack — his face, dark and grim,
> Grows gentle with memories tender,
> And he mutters a prayer for the children asleep,
> For their mother — may Heaven defend her!"

"He passes the fountain, the blasted pine-tree —
  The footstep is lagging and weary;
Yet onward he goes, through the broad belt of light,
  Toward the shades of the forest so dreary.
Hark! was it the night-wind that rustled the leaves?
  Was it moonlight so suddenly flashing?
It looked like a rifle.   'Ha! Mary, good-by!' —
  And the life-blood is ebbing and plashing.

"All quiet along the Potomac to-night;
  No sound save the rush of the river;
While soft falls the dew on the face of the dead —
  The picket's off duty forever!"

CHAPTER XII.

FROM SHILOH TO APPOMATTOX.

ON a certain July morning in the year 1863 three young fellows in their early teens walked into a yet scarcely-awakened Connecticut village. They were on a short vacation tramp between New York and Boston, stiffening their muscles and strengthening their legs as a preparation, it might be, for that real marching that all young fellows of those stirring war-times hoped or expected some day to do on Southern battlefields. For two days they had heard but little of the outside world. Twenty-seven years ago tidings from abroad did not penetrate the country sections as speedily as now. And these lads were so anxious for news! How could it be otherwise with them? They were wide-awake New York boys steeped in the seething excitements of those restless days when all America seemed to live from day to day upon the anxious seat.

Suddenly, as they passed a yet unopened house, one of the boys spied a discarded newspaper of the previous day lying where it had been thrown aside upon the trim green lawn. Instinctively they all stole in and confiscated the vagrant sheet. And as one unfolded it and the others peered over his shoulder all three gave a shout of joy: "The Great Union Victory at Gettysburg!" "Vicksburg Ours!" Here was news indeed. Exultant and thankful the three lads laid down the borrowed newspaper and went their way with swinging steps and lightened hearts, prouder than ever of the boys at the front, with whom they hoped some day to cast in their lot.

It was indeed great news for all the North. The greatest from Sumter to Appomattox. For Gettysburg and Vicksburg marked the turning-point of the war. And yet not the greatest. There was one occurrence, not military indeed but national, that hastened results more than any other achievement. It was a simple dip into the inkstand, a single act of justice. But when Abraham Lincoln laid down the pen that signed the immortal proclamation of emancipation the days of rebellion were numbered. The Edict of Freedom was America's masterstroke.

But those who in Northern homes watched and waited in those troublous times, finding criticism so easy, patience so hard, did not then appreciate to the full the importance of this greatest state paper of the century. To those eager boys Gettysburg and Vicksburg meant more than any presidential proclamation. And so to all the North the tidings from Gettysburg and Vicksburg were both welcome and wonderful.

When the conflict that had raged so furiously through three terrible days gained its first note of victory from the wonderful charge of Stannard's brave brigade and closed with the bloody repulse of Pickett's magnificent charge on Cemetery Ridge the tide of rebel invasion was swept backward from the Pennsylvania hills and the greatest stroke of the Confederacy was brought to naught.

At that very moment that Gibbon was holding the ridge at Gettysburg, and, with a loss of half his force, hurled back the last effort of invasion, Grant, outside the ramparts of far-off Vicksburg, was writing to Pemberton the rebel commander: "I have no terms but the unconditional surrender of the city and garrison." The Fourth of July, 1863, was a notable national holiday. For on that anniversary of American Independence the might of American freemen was fully asserted — the last great attempt of rebellion at invasion was thwarted and the Mississippi was made free from the Lakes to the Gulf.

In both these pivotal happenings the American Soldier was at once the cause and instrument. For this he had labored through many weary months, for this he had gone through all the hard routine of drill and discipline, for this he had borne the brunt at Shiloh and gone through the terrible experience of the Seven Days' Battle in Virginia swamps, for this had he closed in hand-to-hand fight at Perrysville and turned at bay on Malvern Hill, for this had he stood the test at Murfreesboro' and Antietam. East and West had worked and struggled toward victory. To East and West at almost the same hour had come the glorious consummation.

But through how much of heart-ache and despondency,

through how much defeat and disaster had this outlook toward peace been reached. From Shiloh to Gettysburg had been, indeed, a hard road to travel.

And yet there had been but little wavering in will, there had been no shrinkage in the determination to win. Through all

CHARGE OF STANNARD'S BRIGADE AT GETTYSBURG.

these days of delay and inaction, of impatience and expectation, of doubtful battle and balked endeavor, of incompetency in leadership and division in council the baffled North again and again had sent its reinforcements to the field. Tramp! tramp! tramp! with firm and measured tread, steadily, solidly, ceaselessly, from every Northern State the soldiers of the Union set their faces southward, dispatched for the strengthening of their brethren at the front. Tramp! tramp! tramp! in all the mechanical evolutions of review and drill, of advance and retreat and the charge of desperate battle the blue coats all along that shifting death line that stretched from the Mississippi to the sea marched and countermarched, fought and fell.

And still more men were needed. The cause of war was as insatiate as was that horse-leech of whom Scripture tells, who "hath two daughters whose only cry is: Give, give, give!" South as well as North this cry for fresh blood rang out again and again; South as well as North the fighters fell into line until it seemed to those who watched at home as if none would be left as bread-winners when so many went away.

To the first call of President Lincoln on April 15, 1861, for 75,000 men, the enthusiasm inspired by Sumter's fall yielded at once an hundred thousand in reply. The later calls of May and July, 1861, for 500,000 men brought the Government nearly 700,000 in response. And yet, with the next year, came another call for 300,000 volunteers and from every quarter they rallied by thousands while, of those already in service, other thousands re-enlisted "for three years or the war."

The verses of that unknown author whose measures found an echo in many a loyal heart recall to us the steady outpour of Northern vigor that came as the answer to the president's call of July, 1862:

> "We are coming, Father Abraham, three hundred thousand more,
> From Mississippi's winding stream and from New England's shore;
> We leave our ploughs and workshops, our wives and children dear,
> With hearts too full for utterance, with but a silent tear;
> We dare not look behind us, but steadfastly before:
> We are coming, Father Abraham, three hundred thousand more!

"If you look across the hilltops that meet the Northern sky,
Long moving lines of rising dust your vision may descry;
And now the wind, an instant, tears the cloudy veil aside,
And floats aloft our spangled flag in glory and in pride,
And bayonets in the sunlight gleam, and bands brave music pour :
We are coming, Father Abraham, three hundred thousand more !

"If you look all up our valleys where the growing harvests shine,
You may see our sturdy farmer boys fast forming into line ;
And children from their mother's knees are pulling at the weeds,
And learning how to reap and sow against their country's needs;
And a farewell group stands weeping at every cottage door :
We are coming, Father Abraham, three hundred thousand more !

"You have called us and we're coming, by Richmond's bloody tide,
To lay us down, for Freedom's sake, our brothers' bones beside,
Or from foul treason's savage grasp to wrench the murderous blade,
And in the face of foreign foes its fragments to parade.
Six hundred thousand loyal men and true have gone before :
We are coming, Father Abraham, three hundred thousand more ! "

Six hundred thousand loyal men and true *had* gone before. In the spring of 1862 a force of 637,126 men was in the service of the Union, but the waste of this gallant force by the guns of the enemy and by that still deadlier foe — disease — had not been offset by successive battle. The ill-fortune of the Union arms through 1862 made still more troops necessary and the August call for yet another three hundred thousand men taxed alike the patience and the patriotism, the resources and the conscience of the loyal North.

"The defeat of the Confederate Army at Gettysburg and the capture of Vicksburg," says General Sherman, "should have ended the civil war — but no! the leaders demanded the 'last ditch' and their followers seemed willing." And so the war went on. New levies of troops were called for, new enlistments ordered; to McClellan the dilatory drill-master succeeded at length Grant "the hammerer," and the blue and the gray closed in the last desperate struggle for supremacy.

It was not all young blood alone that responded to these later calls. In 1863 a regiment went from Iowa known as "the gray-beard regiment," not a man of which was under forty-five and many in which were over sixty years of age. It was said of this "gray-beard regiment" that they had already contributed fourteen hundred sons and grandsons to the war.

In the long period of conflict — a period stretching from the fall of Sumter on the fifteenth of April, 1861, to the death of Lincoln on the fourteenth of April, 1865, four years to a day — the number of men recruited for the service of the United States was 2,690,401; the number enrolled in the armies of the Confederacy has never been fairly determined, but was at least a million and a half. For the first years of the war, as we have seen, recruiting was spontaneous and enthusiastic, but as the conflict "strung out" to its close the call for volunteers was less generously responded to until at the last service in the North was only obtainable through an ineffectual draft and the payment of large sums of money in "bounties" — a premium for enlistment, and in the South by a sweeping conscription of all white men resident in the Confederacy between the ages of sixteen and sixty — a measure of which it was remarked that the Confederates were robbing the cradle and the grave to fill their armies.

The four million Americans who took up arms for or against the government of the United States may be classed under three general heads — the "hurrah" boys, the duty soldiers and the purchase-money men. To these should properly be added the conscripts, North and South — soldiers against their will, who marched in spite of themselves and fought under protest.

The smoke of Sumter lingered long in the air but, gradually, the reckless enthusiasm of the early days of the conflict subsided into a stern sense of duty. To enlist "just for the fun of it" became less and less frequent and men sought the recruiting office because they felt that they must rather than from a mere love of fighting.

And yet it was these "duty soldiers" who gave strength to the national cause and showed by a sacrifice of life to conscience that the end could only come in victory for the Union.

> "I think about the dear, brave boys
>   My mates in other years,
> Who pine for home and those they love,
>   Till I am choked with tears.
> With shouts and cheers they marched away
>   On glory's shining track,
> But ah! how long, how long they stay —
>   How few of them come back!
>
> "And when I kneel and try to pray,
>   My thoughts are never free,
> But cling to those who toil and fight
>   And die for you and me.
> And when I pray for victory,
>   It seems almost a sin
> To fold my hands and ask for what
>   I will not help to win."

Such men as this, struggling with the two-sided question of duty generally found their way at last to the recruiting office and helped to win the victory for which they had prayed.

And at last through blood and tears "glory's shining track" led on to victory. The "great hammerer" (as Grant has well been called) with the strength of a nation behind him and veteran fighters at his command finally beat down the weakening cause of rebellion and closed at Appomattox in generous

"DO YOU WANT TO LIVE FOREVER?"

conditions to a conquered foe the four long years of stubborn strife.

Who can rightly sum up in few words the heroisms and the valor of those days of struggle? They were exhibited in every small encounter, they were displayed in every mighty battle. Neither side could claim the monopoly of bravery. The War for Secession was a revelation to the world of American courage, American pluck and American endurance. The bloody angle at Spottsylvania, the "slaughter pen" on the slope of Little Round Top at Gettysburg, the "hornet's nest" at Shiloh, the last grand dash at Chickamauga — these and countless other places of crisis and posts of danger stand in the memory of those who yet survive as proof of the courage and persistence of the American soldier.

And so from Bull Run to Shiloh, from Shiloh on to Gettysburg and Appomattox the "cruel war" went on — with defeat here, with victory there, with plans frustrated one day and realized the next, with reconnaissance and sortie, with artillery duels and hand-to-hand encounters, with the "ping" of bullets from the rifle pits and the unrecorded romances of the picket line, with the furious charge, the death-clamber over hostile ramparts, the battle, the capture, the prison-pen and escape, until at last came the end and the furled flags and the silent cannon told that the conflict between brothers was over and that the brave men, North and South, were brothers indeed once more.

Not all the fighters in blue were Hectors, nor was every one in gray an Achilles. Though there is an inspiration in valor, heroism is not always "catching." Cowardice is as old as Cain and while time calls for tests of bravery so long will there be those who flinch before the test. It is a mistake to suppose that soldiers dash into battle with avidity or double-quick to a charge without a tremor. Many a time have the fighters needed to be fairly driven into fight, as even a blooded racer may balk before a five-barred gate. "Come on, come on, my men!" cried a fiery rebel colonel at Malvern Hill, as before a charge his men seemed to hesitate; "what are you waiting for? Do you want to live forever? In with you!" and "in" they went. Over the wires once went the facetious dispatch of the observant operator: "The Seventeenth Pennsylvania Cavalry just passed here, furiously charging to the rear."

Many a private's knee shook when the order "Fall in, men!" came and he knew a battle was at hand; more than one boaster, valiant only at mess, has dived into hiding as with shriek and whirr the deadly shell has cut the air above him, as certain that his doom was its mission as was poor Darky Bill, the company cook, who declared that every shell that sent him "kiting" into cover was shrieking: "Ah-h-h, where's dat nigger! where's dat nigger! *where's* dat nigger!"

Civilians do not have a monopoly of terror and the men that "skedaddled" before Morgan's picturesque raid in the North and Sherman's historic "bummers" in the South sometimes wore uniforms and carried sword and musket.

For not alone does the occasional private show the white feather. The weakness of knees has sometimes been known to affect also the officer, whom favoritism or official patronage has put in command of men braver than he. "Why don't you get behind a tree, Jim?" shouted one private to another as, in one of the Virginia battles, the "zip" of the flying balls sent many a man dodging for shelter. "Tree!" yelled the unsheltered private; "confound it! There ain't enough for the officers."

There were "weak-kneed brothers" and "number one" outlookers in every regiment. Worse than these, there were deserters on both sides, there were cravens and skulkers and "bounty-jumpers," as in every community the bad find place among the good and God's cleansing rain falls alike on just and unjust. But discipline conquers insubordination and brings even timidity steadily into line. The men who fought from a sense

MORGAN'S RAIDERS.

of duty far outnumbered those who were weak of heart or treacherous in faith. And these won the victories.

"There is something grand," says the drummer-boy Harry Kieffer in his sprightly recollections, "in the promptitude with which the order to 'fall in' is obeyed. Every man is at his post. Forcing its way as best it can through the tangled undergrowth of briers and bushes, across ravines and through swamps, our whole magnificent line advances, until after a half-hour's steady work, we reach the skirmish line, which, hardly pressed, falls back into the advancing column of blue as it reaches a little clearing in the forest."

The heroes of that greatest of great rebellions were many. To name them would need a volume, to set down the deeds of valor done would be but an endless repetition of heroisms. How could we even commence the list? Grant the general, "the commander that never took a step backward;" Sherman the persistent; McClellan the matchless engineer; Sheridan the fiery rider; Hancock "the superb;" Custer with the heart of flame; Kearney "who knew not to yield" and Thomas the "rock of Chickamauga," according to Greeley "the greatest soldier of them all." Every patriot at the North had his favorite to cheer to the echo or to run into the current "patter-songs" of the day. And even yet history cannot weigh reputations perfectly nor say who was "best" among them all. And on the other side the line — how shall that roll be fitly commenced — Lee, recreant but royal, perhaps, all things considered, the greatest leader that ever generaled a lost cause — fighting ever a losing battle, prolific in device, masterly in execution; Albert Sidney Johnston, a gallant soldier, a born leader, who died on the field of Shiloh, a martyr to his own indomitable energy; "Stonewall" Jackson, "Lee's right arm," rapid, bewildering, magnetic; Polk, "priest and warrior;" Stuart, perhaps the best cavalryman America has ever produced and a thousand others mistaken in judgment, brave in action — American soldiers all.

And, following their leaders, from the ranks on either side a countless host emerges — brothers in bravery as in speech, if foemen in the hour of fight.

A driver in the regular artillery, shot through the body at Olustee, with his life blood streaming from this mortal wound, struggled to extricate his team from the deadly tangle and to carry off his gun until, his strength not being equal to his valor, he fell dead in the resolute but vain attempt.

And in that same Olustee fight, the rebel lieutenant Colquitt was a conspicuous object to the troops on both sides as, galloping in front of the Confederate ranks, he waved a battle flag and exhorted the men to stand fast and not to lie down or shelter themselves lest the enemy should suppose they had broken.

In Russell's brilliant charge on the redoubts of the Rappahannock Sergeant Roberts of the Sixth Maine was first inside the works. Finding himself alone he deemed discretion the better part of valor and cried out " I surrender." But, turning, he saw his comrades tumbling over the parapet. "No, no; I take it back!" he yelled, made a dash for the rebel colors and captured them.

Colonel Terry, the Texas crack shot, coolly aiming his piece, dropped the United States flag at Fairfax Court House by cutting the halyards with a rifle shot, dashed into the mélée and carried off the flag.

At Spottsylvania Corporal Weeks captured, all unaided, the rebel colors and their guard of six lusty Confederates, and on the same bloody day Sergeant Fasnacht performed precisely the same feat with the single argument of an empty musket. On the official list of those to whom medals of honor were awarded for bravery during the war of the rebellion two hundred and eighty-six men in the ranks were honored for this same dangerous action — gallantry in the capture of the enemy's flag.

In Sheridan's great Richmond raid the First North Carolina charged the Sixth New York battery. In the crush and struggle a Confederate officer cut his way straight to the rear piece and laying his hand on the gun exclaimed: "This is my piece." "Not by a darned sight," replied a New York cannonier, leaping on his gun as with a "scientific" blow from the shoulder he planted his fist between the eyes of the rebel colonel, knocked him off his horse and took him prisoner.

At that brief but bloody fight at Olustee, already referred to, Colonel Fribley's colored troops met the enemy at short range though they had never had a day's experience in loading and firing. "Old troops," says General Hawley, "finding themselves so greatly overmatched, would have run a little and re-formed — with or without orders. The black men stood to be killed or wounded — losing more than three hundred out of five hundred and fifty men."

Bravery in battle is heralded far and wide, repaid with the medal of honor and the applause of a hero-loving world. But there is a moral bravery greater even than that which faces cannons or springs forward to the deadly charge. Such was the conduct of that Ohio regiment left without supplies, suffering for food, desperate enough to appropriate anything that should come in their way. In the dead of night they hear the rumble of wagon wheels. "Grub!" they yell, alive with the joy of approaching relief, and springing into the road stand ready to help unload. But the heavy wagon goes straight on without stopping. Furious at such neglect a dozen strong hands catch at the horses' heads, a swarm of blue-coats clamber into the wagon. Down tumble the supplies; off go the heads of barrels, the tops of cracker boxes. Hunger stops at nothing. "Not for us, eh?" comes the indignant cry in response to the threats and appeals of the drivers. "Well, I guess! Nobody else is going to have this. We're hungry enough to eat you and your horses." "But, boys, boys! for God's sake hold on," the overpowered driver cries. "This grub is for the —— Wisconsin fellows below you. They have been without food twenty-four hours longer than you have. They're starving!" Without a word, with scarcely a moment's hesitation, box-lids are hammered down, supplies reloaded and the hungry heroes with a parting cheer send on the load untouched to those whose necessity is even greater than theirs.

AFTER THE BATTLE.

In May, 1863, a force of rebel cavalry swooping down on Stoneman's advance captured Lieutenant Paine of the First Maine cavalry and his men. While crossing a rapid stream with the prisoners Lieutenant Henry, the commander of the rebel force, was suddenly swept from his horse by the rushing water. No hand among his own men was lifted to save him, but, quick as a flash, the Yankee prisoner, Paine, sprang from his horse, seized his drowning foeman by the collar and swam with him to the shore. For this act of heroism General Fitzhugh Lee gave Paine his liberty without parole or condition and, such are the strange conditions of war, the plucky Yankee lieutenant on reaching Washington found the rebel lieutenant whose life he had saved a prisoner in the Old Capitol prison and there again befriended him.

And Bayard Wilkeson — the Sidney of the war — let his name have place in this all too brief suggestion of brave deeds. Scarcely more than a boy, only nineteen, he held his command — Battery G Fourth U. S. Artillery, of which he was lieutenant — in an exposed position on the Union right at Gettysburg until the rebel General Gordon ordered two batteries to train every gun upon him. Then desperately wounded, Wilkeson fell from his horse and dragged himself into the rebel lines. There, lying wounded to the death, he asked for water. A canteen was brought him but as he took it a wounded soldier, probably one of the enemy, saw it and cried: "For God's sake give me some." The young hero passed the canteen untouched to the sufferer who greedily drank every drop. Then Wilkeson, courteous to the end, smiled on the man, turned slightly and died. Rightly named; Bayard in truth; not even the old cavalier of far-off days *sans peur et sans reproche* did ever a nobler or more knightly deed.

But why increase the list? There have been heroes in every conflict as there are brave men always, as well in peace as war, but the annals of that bloody war for secession are emphasized throughout by valor and punctuated with heroism:

"Oh, not alone the hoary Past
  Spilled precious princely blood;
Oh, not alone its sons were cast
  In knightly form and mood;

Perennial smells of sacrifice
    Make sweet our sickened air;
And truth as leal as Sidney's, lies
    Around us everywhere.

"Renown stands mute beside the graves
    With which the land is scarred;
Unheralded our splendid braves
    Went forth unto the Lord;
No poet hoards their humble names
    In his immortal scrolls,
But none the less the darkness flames
    With their clear-shining souls."

Courage, it used to be asserted, was the cheapest thing in the Army of the Potomac, but so too was it equally common in the army of the center and the army of the west. Of physical courage and contempt of death, says Rossiter Johnson, "no generation of Americans has shown any lack. From Louisburg to Petersburg — a hundred and twenty years, the full span of four generations — they have stood to their guns and been shot down in greater comparative numbers than any other race on earth." Wearied and disheartened but plucky to the last the Confederate soldier made his homely butternut the badge of bravery and shed about a lost and desperate cause the halo of a deathless valor; stern and unyielding and never despairing of the right, the boys in blue glorified the hour of victory by their kindly helpfulness toward a fallen foe and by their mighty achievements made the name and the power of the American Republic honored and feared throughout the world.

The last stand had been made, the last blow given, the last dashing charge attempted and repelled. With Appomattox the war ended. And the picture that General Porter draws so vividly may apply with equal truth to all the opposing forces that with folded banners drew backward, one to the North the other to the South, from that wavering death-line that had stretched for so many months from the sierras to the sea: "The charges were withdrawn from the guns, the camp-fires were left to smoulder in their ashes, the flags were tenderly furled — those historic banners, battle-stained, bullet-riddled, many of them but remnants of their former selves with scarcely enough left of them on which to imprint the names of the battles they had seen — and the Army of the Union and the Army of Northern Virginia, turned their backs upon each other for the first time in four long, bloody years."

CHAPTER XIII.

BOOTS AND SADDLE.

HOME again! The gallant but hopeless defense of Richmond, which has given to Lee's wasted line the right to the name of heroes, had ended in the surrender at Appomattox and the war was over. The armies of the conqueror and the conquered were disbanded or melted away, peace at last rested upon the land and the soldiers, North and South, became once again citizens and bread-winners.

Six hundred thousand lives and six thousand million dollars had been the cost in blood and treasure at which the conflict had been waged; but it had made the United States a nation and had put to rest forever the terror of civil war.

Quickly the work of disbanding went on. The great reviews of the twenty-third and the twenty-fourth of May, 1865, when, first, the Army of the Potomac and, next, the Army that, led by Sherman, had made its historic march to the sea and "swung around the circle" of the Confederacy marched in close column, twenty-four deep, around the gleaming Capitol and down Pennsylvania Avenue to the reviewing stand at the White House. Two hundred thousand men and more, bronzed of face but with a free and steady step and the elastic spring which only the veteran soldier knows — the remnants of mighty regiments, their smoke-stained battle-flags torn by wind and fight, they marched in grand review before the President of the United States and the chiefs of the nation. The president — but not *their* president! Not the one man of royal soul and of homely face who through four weary years of war had never faltered, never despaired, but had worked steadily on for the end he knew would come, the end that now the grand review, the throbbing music of regimental bands, the streaming banners, the thronging streets of Washington welcomed with so much of pomp and exultation. Their captain — their president — where was he? "He had lived to enter the enemy's capital, lived to see the authority of the United States restored over the whole country and then was snatched away, when the people were as much as ever in need of his genius for the solution of new problems that suddenly confronted them."

How many a soldier in that great review, missing the kindly face, the rugged features, the gaunt, ungainly frame that were as familiar as they were dear to all loyal Americans, felt as did the most American of all our American poets* when, out of the anguish of his soul, he wrote his grandest verse "My Captain":

---

* Walt Whitman, whom Sir Edwin Arnold describes as "that grand old poet of yours whom America does not seem to appreciate."

> "O Captain! my Captain! our fearful trip is done;
> The ship has weather'd every rack, the prize we sought is won;
> The port is near, the bells I hear, the people all exulting,
> While follow eyes the steady keel, the vessel grim and daring;
>   But O heart! heart! heart!
>   O the bleeding drops of red,
>   Where on the deck my Captain lies,
>   Fallen cold and dead!
>
> "O Captain! my Captain! rise up and hear the bells;
> Rise up — for you the flag is flung — for you the bugle trills;
> For you bouquets and ribbon'd wreaths — for you the shores a-crowding;
> For you they call, the swaying mass, their eager faces turning;
>   Here, Captain! dear father!
>   This arm beneath your head;
>   It is some dream that on the deck
>   You've fallen cold and dead.
>
> "My Captain does not answer, his lips are pale and still;
> My father does not feel my arm, he has no pulse nor will;
> The ship is anchor'd safe and sound, its voyage closed and done,
> From fearful trip the victor ship comes in with object won.
>   Exult, O shores, and ring, O bells!
>   But I with mournful tread,
>   Walk the deck my Captain lies,
>   Fallen cold and dead."

The soldiers of the blue went home to welcoming throngs, gay flaunting banners, cheers and shouts of "Well done!" The soldiers of the gray — that gray faded almost out of remembrance, tattered and travel-torn almost beyond repair — went home to welcomes just as warm. They may have met regrets and murmurings perhaps over the end that had been defeat, but it was defeat bravely kept at bay through many bitter months; and so, after all, the home-coming of the Southern soldier was a time of happiness and of joy to the war-spent veterans who had left their arms and artillery parked and stacked at Appomattox, at Raleigh, or at Shreveport and had taken nothing to their homes but their well-worn uniforms and a sense of duty — as they had understood it — valiantly done.

The ravages of war had worked havoc in many a gallant command. Every Northern regiment had lost heavily in battle and yet more heavily under the fell hand of disease. Of the Fourth Iowa Infantry, comprising thirteen hundred men, fully

THE HOME-COMING OF THE SOUTHERN SOLDIERS.

one thousand had laid down their lives for their country. Of the Fifth Iowa Infantry which enlisted with 967 men and officers and received 70 recruits, 89 were killed in battle, 90 died of disease, 281 were wounded, 221 broken in health were discharged for disability and 96 were captured only to die of neglect in rebel prisons — a terrible tale of loss. These figures could be paralleled by the records of every State and not a veteran, back from the wars, but brought with him tender memories of comrades left behind and of nameless graves scattered all over the sunny South. That officers' reunion so delicately pictured by Major Halpine could find its counterpart in many an after-war celebration:

> "Three years ago to-day
>   We raised our hands to heaven,
> And on the rolls of muster
>   Our names were thirty-seven;
> There were just a thousand bayonets,
>   And the swords were thirty-seven,
> And we took the oath of service
>   With our right hands raised to heaven.
>
> "Oh! 'twas a gallant day,
>   In memory still adored,
> That day of our sun-bright nuptials
>   With the musket and the sword!
> Shrill rang the fifes, the bugles blared,
>   And beneath a cloudless heaven
> Twinkled a thousand bayonets,
>   And the swords were thirty-seven.
>
> "Of the thousand stalwart bayonets
>   Two hundred march to-day;
> Hundreds lie in Virginia swamps,
>   And hundreds in Maryland clay;
> And other hundreds, less happy, drag
>   Their shattered limbs around,
> And envy the deep, long, blessed sleep
>   Of the battle-field's holy ground.
>
> "For the swords — one night, a week ago,
>   The remnant, just eleven,
> Gathered around a banqueting board
>   With seats for thirty-seven;

> There were two limped in on crutches,
>   And two had each but a hand
> To pour the wine and raise the cup
>   As we toasted 'Our flag and land!'
>
> "And the room seemed filled with whispers
>   As we looked at the vacant seats,
> And, with choking throats, we pushed aside
>   The rich but untasted meats;
> Then in silence we brimmed our glasses,
>   As we rose up — just eleven —
> And bowed as we drank to the loved and the dead
>   Who had made us thirty-seven!"

Within six months after the fall of the Confederacy the million or more soldiers of the Union had returned to their homes. The vast Volunteer Army of the United States was a thing of the past. The regular army being a national organization was still kept at its full standard of fifty thousand men and was employed in garrison duty and post service in the South and West. The United States was divided into five Military Divisions and these were subdivided into nineteen Departments. Among these departments the standing army of the United States was distributed.

Foreign nations had declared that so large a force of armed men could not be disbanded without trouble and possible anarchy. Events proved the falsity of this prophecy and the reaction of restlessness that is to be looked for after every great war found expression in but two brief and purposeless eruptions — the "Fenian" excitement of 1866 and the "Ku-Klux" disorders of 1867-69. Both were erratic, both were foolhardy and, to a certain degree, picturesque. Both called for military intervention to overawe and disintegrate them and neither of them were in step with the desires or the spirit of the American people.

General Thomas W. Sweeney, the leading spirit in the Fenian Invasion of Canada in 1866, was a brave and dashing American soldier. He had lost an arm at Cherubusco, while serving under Scott in Mexico; he had in 1851 held Fort Yuma in California against a large Indian force, though he and his men were at starvation's door; he had bravely kept his charge of the United States arsenal in St. Louis, with but forty men, against three thousand clamorous Secessionists saying: "I'll blow it up and you with it before I surrender; there are only forty of us to die!" he had served under Grant at Donelson and been made a brigadier-general for his bravery in the war.

With Sweeney in the Canadian invasion of 1866 were other veteran soldiers, filled with Irish enthusiasm and hatred of England. But the United States, wisely, was true to her treaty-promises. General Meade and a sufficient force were dispatched to the border, the invader's supplies were cut off and the adventurers finally surrendered to the power of the United States. A later Fenian outbreak in 1870 was repelled by the Canadian militia and scattered by a United States marshal.

The Southern restlessness was more serious because more secret. Dissatisfied men, rendered venomous by defeat and angered by the seeming inequalities of "reconstruction" sought to reverse the decision of the war, to terrorize the negro and keep Northern life and capital from the land that so needed this aid to right development. With a secrecy and an organization that smacked of mediæval barbarism they banded together under an oath more picturesque than practical: "I swear that by daylight and darkness, at all times and on all occasions, the steel shall pay the debt of steel, the lead shall recompense for lead, the Southern Cross shall yet defy the world!"

There was much more to the same effect, but the valor that skulks in the shadow and strikes in the dark is the weakest sort of courage and usually comes to grief. Under vigorous measures and the presence of the United States soldier in the disturbed sections the attempt at an American vendetta was stamped out and the K. K. K. is now only a phase of the picturesque lunacies of America.

So too in the reconstruction troubles through which the Southern States had naturally to pass before entire peace and unimpeded law were restored the soldiers of the United States called repeatedly to unquiet sections, established the national authority and brought rest to the yet disorganized communities.

Gradually the East grew quiet; the after-grumblings of strife were stilled; the ravages of war were charitably covered over by a growing respect between men and by the healing forces of nature. Only in the West was there disquiet and unrest. There cavalrymen became hunters and soldiers scouts as the musket and sword that had conquered on Southern battle-fields were turned against the red-men of the plains, the cañons and the lava beds.

For years the Indians of the far West have been the tool and sport of American mismanagement. Injustice always breeds discontent and this, in the simple mind, leads to a desire for revenge. The barbarian is ever a child and must strike when struck or abuse when abused. So Navajo and Piegan, Apache and Modoc, Sioux and Nez Percé and Ute, tricked in trade, robbed by agents, worried by settlers, alternately cajoled and threatened, petted and harried, have turned protests into

CUSTER'S LAST STAND.

uprisings and pleas into massacres until alike good and bad have fallen beneath their vengeance, the army has been kept on the alert and the red-man himself, always defeated, is becoming more and more a dependent and a serf.

From the Apache and Cheyenne troubles of 1863 and '64 until the successful policy of General Crook in 1883, the twenty years of frontier trouble have been full of peril, of action and of blood.

The Indian policy of the Government has been fickle, illiberal, faithless and bad, the moral influence of the soldiers upon the red-men has been of the worst character, the military rule to which they have been subjected has been autocratic, tyrannical and full of harm, and the Indian wars of the United States have been, largely, of the nation's own making.

But, as has before been shown, the causes of a war do not always govern the character of the fighters in that war and the bravery of the American soldier in his encounters with the "hostiles" of the mountains and the plains has been above criticism, positive and obstinate. Shirland and his California volunteers, the captors of Mangas Colorado the Apache; Chivington and his avengers at the camp of Black Kettle the Cheyenne; Fetterman and his eighty-four regulars making their last tragic stand against two thousand Northern Indians on Lodge Trail Ridge; Powell and his thirty men at bay, but finally defeating with terrible loss Red Cloud and his twenty-five hundred Sioux; Miles and his brave four hundred in the Wolf Mountains; the half-dozen cavalrymen of the gallant Sixth, holding their ground for thirty-six hours against a force of splendidly-mounted Kiowas and Comanches, twenty-five to one; Crook and his plucky New Mexican riders — wherever the bugle has sounded "boots and saddle!" the Indian fighter who wears the blue has proved his right to the name of fighter indeed.

But, in all the sad and sorry story of Indian atrocity and American treachery, of Indian bravery and American valor there is no paragraph more startling, more bloody or more dramatic than is that which tells of the last gallant stand of Custer and his men — the Battle of Little Big Horn.

It is the climax of all Indian warfare from the days of Philip of Pokanoket to those of Sitting Bull the Sioux and Geronimo the Apache, and is all the more absorbing because of the mystery that shrouds it and its hints at desperate valor which, alas! no man of all that brave four hundred lives to prove or disprove.

General George Armstrong Custer of the Seventh U. S. Cavalry was, in many respects, America's *beau sabreur*. The choice of McClellan and the favorite of Sheridan, he was the idol of his own hard-riders and the envy of his Indian foemen. His very appearance was striking and picturesque as, in his broad cavalier's hat, his gold-bedizened jacket and high cavalry boots, with his long yellow hair flying in the wind he would ride like a tornado against rebel cavalry or Indian warrior — a subject worthy Vandyke's pencil, the very type of the dashing trooper of romance.

The war over, he was assigned to duty on the plains and became the most daring and most successful of the Indian fighters of 1870. On the fifteenth of May, 1876, Custer was ordered to lead his regiment, the Seventh Cavalry, as the advance of a joint expedition against the hostile Sioux. On the morning of the twenty-fifth of June, with five companies of his command amounting to not over four hundred men, he fell into a cleverly-arranged ambuscade of the confederated Sioux backed by a force of at least three thousand Indian warriors. A desperate fight ensued. Valiantly holding his ground, vainly looking for the help that came not, stubbornly at bay but calm, cool and courageous to the last Custer fell fighting and his devoted soldiers to a man fell, also fighting, around the body of their chief.

Blinded by a savage ruse, himself the victim of political wiles that had stirred up his fighting blood and driven him to a determination to "make his mark" once more, Custer's unguarded advance and reckless charge were, perhaps, unwise generalship, but they were the chief ingredients of heroism and a dauntless courage and as such have given him an immortality that will ever make him the typical Indian fighter of the nineteenth century. Much is forgiven to valor; a brave man's death covers all mistakes.

Of other instances of soldierly courage in the Indian fights that have become a part of American history since 1865, there are many on record. There is always a fascination to us around the stories of life "among the red-skins," and, ignoring always the Indian's side of the question, we listen with quickened pulse and brightening eyes to the account of how Clark and his forty-eight men held over seven hundred "hostiles" at bay for fully three hours of battle; how Sergeant Taylor at the risk of his life rescued his lieutenant (now Captain Charles King, the soldier-novelist) from Apache arrows, supporting his wounded officer with one arm and with the other managing his deadly carbine; how private John Nihill acted as a "flanker" to his eight comrades of the Fifth Cavalry in the heart of the White-stone mountains and held forty Indians at bay so that his brother-soldiers could escape from the ambush; how Amos Chapman, the scout of the Third Cavalry, leaped across the body of his fallen comrade and held off the circling Comanches until he could "shoulder" the wounded man and bear him out of the death-trap into which he had fallen; how private William Evans, of the Seventh Infantry, at the imminent risk of his life carried dispatches for General Crook through a country inhabited by hostile Sioux, dodging death all the way; how Sergeant William Lewis of the Third Cavalry won a medal from Congress for volunteering to discover the whereabouts of Little Wolf and his Cheyenne warriors — all these we hear with pride as we do the countless other tales of risk and daring, of dash and valor that illumine the otherwise dull details of army life on the plains and make vivid finger-marks on the annals of Indian warfare.

CHAPTER XIV.

THE BOYS OF '98.

FOR thirty-three years the noise of battle had been absent from the land. 1865 had seen the last angry shot of war, and, since Custer's gallant fight in 1876, no Indian hostilities had risen to the importance of battle, while the standing army of the United States, reduced to its minimum of less than twenty-five thousand men, had been little more than an attenuated police force. Some disturbances there had been, such as the Orange riots of 1871, in New York City, the railroad strikes of the Middle and Western states, in 1877, and the imported anarchist plots of a later day, which were quelled only by the law of the bullet and the bayonet; while, in one case at least, the militia of the states showed that, even when the sympathy of the soldier was with the victim of capital's oppression, his duty as an instrument of law and order rose superior to his sympathies. Only the loyalty of the militia and the superb discipline of the regulars kept the two weeks of terror in 1877 from developing into a time of anarchy and mob-domination.

The peaceful work of the soldier in the years since the Rebellion has been of no little value to American life and progress. The great Centennial Exhibition of 1876 was made a marvel of regularity and good order by the directing hand of one of the nation's bravest soldiers, General Hawley of Connecticut. And in the elaborate display made by the United States government at that great exposition, and at the still vaster Columbian Exposition at Chicago in 1893, the part contributed by the War Department was both suggestive and creditable. There were to be seen all the latest developments in military art, guns of every size and style and mounting, pontoons, bridge trains, and army wagons. Cartridge-making went on before the eyes of the spectators, and the exhibits entered by the Engineer Corps and the Signal Service were especially valuable.

From the days of Pike and Long to those of Frémont and the later explorers of our Western lands, the army of the United States has been foremost in expeditions of research and discovery in the remote and unknown sections of the nation's broadening empire. And, in these recent years, the cause of science owes to the brave investigations, under most adverse circumstances, of two gallant American soldiers, Schwatka and Greely, its latest information as to the lands and peoples about the frozen Pole; while it is the army that has opened up to us the exhaustless opportunities of the Philippines, the rich possibilities of Porto Rico, and the rediscovered values of the noble island of Cuba.

This last contribution to American power and possession came through one of the briefest wars on record, in which regular and volunteer grappled with those unknown foes, temperature and climate, in a foreign land; for the first time conducting operations off the mainland of the continent, and taking the soldiers of the Union into distant and unfriendly seas.

The story of the causes and beginnings of what President

McKinley calls "our extraordinary war with Spain" need not be recited here. It was an unavoidable conflict that might have been avoided,—if we can explain that apparently inconsistent expression,—into which the President was forced by the persistence of the newspaper press, the clamor of Congress, and the pressure of the people; all alike brought to a climax by that unfortunate and dastardly deed, the explosion of the battleship *Maine* on February 15, 1898, in the harbor of Havana.

Even that dreadful disaster, while it aroused the indignation and wrath of the American people, did not at once lead to the war that was inevitable. "Suspicion and horror," as President McKinley declared, "stirred the nation's heart profoundly;" but, as in the case of the "shots heard round the world," at Lexington and Concord, the American people did not rush blindly into war, nor did they take up the sword until they had exhausted the means of peace. With a patience that was surprising, and the true Anglo-Saxon love of fair play, they awaited the report of the Naval Board of Inquiry as to the cause of the destruction of the *Maine*, while at the same time awaiting some result from the shadowy plans proposed by Spain for the relief of the persecuted people of Cuba.

The report was as unsatisfactory as the reform. The Board of Inquiry declared that the *Maine* was blown up by a submarine mine, but made no direct charge against Spain; the reform promised in Cuba amounted to nothing; and, urged on by the people and by the Congress, who unanimously voted a "defense appropriation" of fifty million dollars, the President recognized at last the necessity for final decision and action. He therefore declared that "in the name of humanity, in the name of civilization, in behalf of endangered American interests, which give us the right and the duty to speak and act, the war in Cuba must stop."

Peaceful measures had been of no avail. As in the greater strife for Union, thirty-seven years before, the words of Cutter's noble poem rang true again:

> "Lo, brightly o'er the breaking day shines Freedom's holy star;
> Peace cannot cure the sickly time. All hail the healer, War!"

The healer came quickly. Responding to the President's message of April 11, 1898, Congress, on the 19th of April, voted to interfere in the strife in Cuba, and Spain was told to "withdraw" from the island. The Spanish Minister refused to remain in Washington, and left at once; while the American Minister at Madrid was practically told to "get out."

This action, under the rulings of international law, meant that Spain had declared war. This date was the 21st of April; and that is the date which will go into American history as the beginning of the war of 1898.

The very next day the President of the United States announced the existence of a state of war, declared a blockade of Cuban ports, and on the 22d called for 125,000 volunteers. To this call almost ten men responded where but one could be taken; a second call for 75,000 was made on May 25, and with the regular army increased to 60,000 men, the United States regulars and the United States volunteers prepared to enforce the demands of the republic in the cause of justice, humanity, and right.

The navy had been proportionately and speedily increased, and for a time it appeared as though the war was to be a naval rather than a land conflict. But opportunity came at last, as after long but necessary delay the navy cleared the path by locating and bottling up Cervera's fleet, which had given a scare to the whole Atlantic coast, from the day it sailed from the Cape Verde Islands and lost itself, to the morning that Schley saw it and locked it up in Santiago harbor.

This changed the course of the war. Instead of assaulting Havana, or occupying Porto Rico as a base of supplies for a fall campaign against Cuba, the sudden determination was made to launch an army against Santiago from the rear, and by a union of action with the navy at the front to close in and crush or capture alike the army and fleet of Spain at Santiago.

This was to be the first move. In case this success did not at once end the war, then a fall campaign against Havana was to be organized, which would call into service all the volunteer regiments who in camps of instruction or of concentration were being drilled into fighting material for this greater campaign, if it should come.

So the Fifth Army Corps, concentrated at the camp at Tampa in Florida, was ordered to Cuba. The command was given to Major-General William R. Shafter, a rough and ready veteran of the Civil War, who was selected for the leadership because General Miles, the commanding general of the army, believed him to be just the leader for a short and sharp campaign, in which hardships, though necessary, would be brief, and inconveniences and discomforts would be philosophically accepted as "part of the day's work" by the troops selected for the service.

The troops thus selected were from those especially inured to the chance of hardships, inconvenience, and discomfort — the regular army of the United States, the men who are trained to take things in their course with no thought of what will be said at home, for, too often, their only home is the barracks, their only "father" the colonel. As Mr. Barnes has described the regular: —

> "He takes it all as it may come,
> And it's more of work than play,
> From the goose step into the awkward squad —
> Then into a trench some day.
> He answers 'sir' to his officer,
> He watches his sergeant well,
> And if things they happen to rub him wrong
> He cannot run home and tell."

It was of these "regular fighting men" that the Fifth Corps was largely composed. "In the Fifth Corps," says General Shafter, "I had virtually the whole of the regular army of the United States. That was brought about by the fact that when I left Tampa the volunteer troops were just beginning to arrive, and I had but three regiments of volunteers — the Seventy-first New York, the Second Massachusetts, and the 'Rough Riders,' the latter a regiment which had been raised, as the regular regiments are, by enlistments from Maine to Washington Territory, and the members of which were nearly all inured to the vicissitudes of a soldier's life."

On the fourteenth of June, after numerous setbacks and one false start, the army of invasion got away at last — eight hundred and fifteen officers, sixteen thousand enlisted men, two thousand horses and mules. It was a good army, but weak in many of the necessities of a campaign — no horses for the cavalry, few guns for the artillery, and a lamentable lack of good rifles, smokeless powder, hospital and medical stores, high grade provisions, and, especially, sufficient transports. But then, you see, this was to be a short and sharp campaign, and if things were lacking the "boys" were so anxious to see service that they did but little grumbling and less complaining.

Under convoy of a strong guard of battleships the overloaded transports sailed across a calm and peaceful summer sea, and on the twenty-second of June the American armada set ashore its army of invasion through the tossing surf at Daiquiri, a little village eighteen miles east of Santiago. It was flanked by hills and supplied with the machine shops and pier used in connection with a Spanish-American iron-ore plant.

By boats and launches the men were sent ashore, the horses and mules tossed overboard to swim, and, after the warships by a thorough shelling of the shore had cleared the brush of any lurking Spaniards, the Fifth Army corps found itself at last on Cuban soil, with four "Rough Riders" racing up the hill to fling out the stars and stripes from the deserted and dismantled blockhouse. The army of liberation was at last in Cuba.

General Shafter had outlined a simple and thorough plan of attack which, if quickly carried out, would, he felt, secure the capture of Santiago with but little loss of life and just a taste of hardship.

Three things, however, were somewhat ignored in the general's calculations — the persistent valor of the Spaniard, the perplexing entanglements of a Spanish trail, and the "get there" qualities of the American volunteer.

In the composition of the Rough Riders — officially known as the First United States Volunteer Cavalry — the "get there" quality was very much in evidence. Made up from such enthusiastic elements as the cowboy and frontiersman of the Western prairie and the college-bred athlete of the East, the fight for Santiago seemed to them something in the nature of a cattle roundup or a football rush, in which the best man was he who got in first.

General Shafter's plan was to advance his army by designated divisions along different trails to the Santiago road, but the dismounted cavalry under command of General Wheeler, and of which the Rough Riders were a part, while hunting on the twenty-fourth of June for a suitable camping ground, got far in the lead; there they struck the trail of an ambushed Spanish column, and, with the usual impetuosity of the young American volunteer and the earnestness of the combined cowboy and college athlete, they at once "sailed in" and "did up" that Spanish force in the first land battle of the war.

It was not really a battle. It was scarcely a skirmish. General Shafter calls it "a brush with the Spaniards"; but in the effect it had on the army, the display it made of the fighting qualities of the volunteer, and the spirit of determination it impressed upon the Spaniards who there were driven from the jungle, the cavalry "brush" at Guasimas was as important as it was spirited.

On the thirtieth of June the forward movement was begun. Again General Shafter's plans were somewhat interfered with by Spanish valor and American zeal. He wished to get between the Spanish army and the city, drive them down toward the shore, and there, caught between his army and the fleet, overthrow or capture them.

To do this he sent one division of his army to occupy the little town of El Caney to the north of his headquarters, despatched another division to occupy and hold the heights of San Juan which lay between El Caney and Santiago.

"If I can get the enemy in my front and the city at my back," General Shafter wrote to Admiral Sampson, "I can very soon make them surrender, or drive them toward the Morro."

It was a good plan; but when the division sent to occupy

El Caney reached the town they found it held so persistently by the Spaniards in trench and blockhouse that the "two hours" in which General Lawton felt sure he could "dispose of the Spaniards" at El Caney grew to ten hours before the end was reached.

At the same time the division sent to hold the heights of San Juan waited in the trails and beside the San Juan River for the signal to join with the victorious troops from El Caney and sweep over the heights to the Spanish rear. But the signal did not come, for very good reasons, and the regulars and Rough Riders on the San Juan trail, being exposed to a remorseless Spanish fire, became restless, and on the first indication of a half order for an advance swarmed across the river and rushed the heights.

So, much to General Shafter's regret, two battles were going on at once. "I began to fear," he says, "that I had made a mistake in making two fights in one day, and I sent Major Noble with orders to Lawton to hasten with his troops along the Caney road, placing himself on the right of Wheeler."

But when the major reached Lawton with his message, the general's only order was to point to his black and white regulars just springing to the final charge.

Nothing could restrain them; up the hill they dashed unmindful of the withering fire of the defenders, whom they had fought at long range all day. Up the hill, over the trenches, into the blockhouse, they swept resistlessly, and El Caney was won.

In much the same manner, the regulars and volunteers at the "bloody angle" of the San Juan trail, chafing and restless under their long wait in the range of a persistent and destructive Spanish fire, interpreted literally the words of

General Shafter's aide-de-camp, "the heights must be taken at all hazards," and when their commander pointed to the heights in a sort of half-order, Rough Riders and regulars, white and black, infantry and cavalry, stormed up the San Juan hills. Singly and in bunches, but never in serried ranks, they crawled and raced up first one hill and then another, losing men as they rushed in the face of a desperate Spanish fire, and, at last, panting but proud of their achievement, cruelly decimated but victorious, while dying men played the hero and wounded men refused to go to the rear, they cheered themselves and their comrades, and the heights of San Juan were won.

There they rested, and there they camped. Digging trenches with insufficient material, they faced the Spaniards and held the heights, in spite of strong efforts to urge the general to a withdrawal, and when at last, after Cervera's fleet had been destroyed, the last hope of the Spaniards cut away, and a persistent front maintained in spite of tropical rain and tropical fever, the last shot was fired, the last white flag of truce displayed, and on the fourteenth of July, General Toral, the Spanish commander, surrendered to General Shafter, and the stars and stripes floated above the captured city of Santiago.

"It was a magnificent achievement," says Lieutenant Parker, "with less than thirteen thousand effective fighting men, the Fifth Army Corps captured in twenty days, twenty-eight thousand of the enemy in a fortified city well provisioned and well equipped with all the munitions of war. It conquered for the United States a territory about equal to that of New England, and drove from the safe shelter of a landlocked, mine-defended harbor a formidable fleet of the

AT GUASIMAS.
"Even the wounded would not go to the rear."

enemy, to fall an easy prey to our vigilant and invincible squadron."

It was a good record for the Fifth Army Corps, for the regulars, for the Rough Riders, and the Massachusetts and New York volunteers.

"Santiago," says General Shafter, "has been called a soldier's campaign. There is a great deal of truth in that, but the implication that any important movement or action was taken without orders or forethought is untrue. When the final attack was made on July 1, individual officers and men, and in fact most of the officers and men, distinguished themselves by gallant and intelligent performance of duty. They were intelligent American soldiers; each one was thinking of what he was doing, and not depending for all his thinking on the officers over him. In that respect the soldiers of the American army are superior to those of any other army in the world."

The eastern end of Cuba having been conquered, the next step in the military programme was the occupation of the island of Porto Rico. This campaign General Miles himself took in charge, and on the twenty-fifth of July he landed with an army of less than five thousand men at the port of Guanica, on the south coast of the block-shaped island. Ponce, the chief city of the island, a few miles away, speedily capitulated, and then in four columns, General Miles proceeded to "cover" the whole island and gradually drive the Spanish army of resistance into the capital city of San Juan on the north coast.

The resistance, however, of the Spanish army proved but slight. Without the support of the Porto Ricans, who openly welcomed the Americans, without hope of reënforcements or the help of an assisting fleet, the Spanish army could but make a show of resistance in defence of their "honor," and in all that short campaign there was scarcely an engagement that rose to the dignity of a battle.

Just the same, however, the American army was ready and anxious for such an opportunity and made the most of what little resistance they did encounter at last, as, on the thirteenth of August, they faced at the pass of Aibonito a plucky Spanish commander who dared them to assault his position on the heights; the guns of the battery were unlimbered, planted, charged, and aimed directly at the Spanish works; the gunner sprang back to discharge his piece at the defiant Spaniard. Then a shout was heard; a rider came galloping up, waving a paper.

"Peace, peace!" he cried. "Cease firing; peace has been proclaimed!"

It was the end of the war. Spain's last resistance in America was the bold reply of one plucky colonel, and the American gunner was cheated out of his desired shot.

Off in far-away Manila, however, the news of peace came too late to avoid the long-expected clash. There was no cable communication with America nearer than Hongkong, four hundred miles away. So the news of the signing of the peace protocol at Washington on the thirteenth of August did not reach Manila for several days.

Meanwhile the army and the navy had united for a joint attack. Admiral Dewey was to bombard the forts and batteries outside the town; and under this support General Merritt was to march his army out of Camp Dewey on the beach outside Manila, storm the trenches and the fort, and carry the city by assault.

It was an admirably planned combination, and it succeeded

admirably. The fleet stood across the bay on the morning of the thirteenth of August; and while the bulk of the fleet steamed on to overawe the city by the threat of their presence, the flagship and two cruisers began the bombardment of the old Malate fort, half a mile outside of Manila on the waterfront, and the connecting lines of trenches.

Under cover of this protecting fire, the soldiers filed out of Camp Dewey, volunteers and a few regulars, most of them far-western regiments from Utah to California. With true Western push and audacity they pushed ahead; charged the trenches; carried the moat-encircled fort, and on the staff above the Malate ran up the stars and stripes.

Sheltered by trench and blockhouse, the Spaniards fired on the impulsive Americans; but reënforcements came up; the trenches and blockhouse were carried, and over the last rampart and up the broad and beautiful ocean esplanade, or Lunetta, the troops marched in close order, band playing, and colors flying.

Before them towered the last barrier between them and the town, — the gray old city wall of Manila. Right on the soldiers pressed, watchful for the order to assault. But even as they advanced in parade up the Lunetta, the white flag of surrender streamed from the east bastion of the fortified wall; and General Merritt went into the city to confer with the governor-general.

Soon the surrender came. The Spanish power in the Philippines had fallen; and the American conquerors, marching in through the queer old city gate, ran up " Old Glory " above the governor's palace, and received the surrender of the Spanish army, the city, and the defences.

The assault on Manila was the last battle with Spain. The

news of peace came across the sea, and alike on Atlantic and Pacific shore all hostilities ceased.

Later, unfortunate hostilities broke out in and about Manila between the American possessors of the islands and the impatient and misguided Filipino insurgents. For though the mission of the United States in these islands was first the conquest of the Spanish power, and after that the protection and bettering of the natives, there could not be any question of negotiation for the second until peace and order were secured. Instead, the natives, unwisely led, would have inaugurated a reign of terror, and did precipitate war. But Admiral Dewey and General Otis, in command after the return of General Merritt, were able officers, well fitted to cope with the situation, while the Western and Pennsylvania troops, under Otis's command, displayed a valor and discipline that defeated every Filipino ambush and attack.

> "We sent you o'er the sunlit sea —
>   Men of the West —
> To carry peace and industry
>   To war's unrest.
> No grateful homage found ye there,
>   Nor honor due;
> A sullen land, with threat'ning air,
>   Admitted you.
>
> . . . .
>
> "We trusted, and were not deceived —
>   Men of the West;
> Ye fought and died as ye had lived —
>   Your nation's best.
> And ye who live to toil anew,
>   We trust as well
> As those who, faithful, toiled with you
>   And, faithful, fell."

So ended the war with Spain. The struggle on land was brief, but sharp and decisive, and, as President McKinley said: "There had been many who had tried to avert it, as, on the other hand, there were many who would have precipitated it at an early date. In its prosecution and conclusion the great majority of our countrymen of every section believed they were fighting in a just cause, and at home or at sea, or in the field, they had part in its glorious triumphs.

"It was the war of an undivided nation. Every great act in its progress, from Manila to Santiago, from Guam to Porto Rico, met universal and hearty commendation. The protocol commanded the practically unanimous approval of the American people. It was welcomed by every lover of peace beneath the flag."

To this end, to success and peace, the American soldier, whether fighting on the field or held as a reserve in home camps, equally contributed. The valor of the one and the discipline of the other alike had lot and part in the grand result; and, when giving credit to the regulars at El Caney and the Rough Riders at San Juan, to the skirmishers in Porto Rico and the resistless Westerners on the ramp of the Malate fort, let us also give praise to those who, awaiting orders in camp or assigned to duty in distant and peaceful ports, cheerfully accepted their disappointment, and proved by that same obedience to orders that sent their brothers storming against the trenches of the foe how nobly could all alike — volunteer and regular, black and white, fighter or waiter — sustain and uplift the proud title of the American soldier.

As a people we do not love war. The best generals have been those whose sympathies and inclinations were against bloodshed. Grant and Sheridan, typical soldiers both, had an utter abhorrence of war, and the gallant cavalry leader has been heard to declare that "the time is coming when the killing of a thousand men in battle will be looked upon as a thousand murders."

But, when occasion demanded, these leaders were quick in action, furious in battle, relentless in methods. War is no parlor play; it is terrible, repulsive, brutalizing. But horrible as it is, it has been a factor in the world's enlightenment; barbarous as it appears, it has been an instrument for the world's refinement. Duty sometimes compels to desperate deeds, and when such occasion arises the fiercest fighter is the strongest inducement toward peace.

It is said that in the ranks of the Confederate army there was one soldier, at least, who sought to wage a bloodless war. He was a member of the Forty-first Georgia Regiment. He was in every battle fought by his regiment, in every skirmish in which his company was engaged, in every charge made by his command, but he never fired his gun. He had conscientious scruples against bloodshed, though none against armed aggression. He simply did not believe in killing men. He frequently charged the enemy with a yell, and saw his comrades fall by his side, but whether routing the Union soldiers or being routed by them he would not shoot. He was always ready for duty — stood guard, remained at the picket post, and obeyed implicitly every command of his superior officers except to draw cartridges, load his gun and shoot.

Had the armies been composed throughout of such material, of course no result could have been reached. To fight to conquer is to fight to kill.

And so, whatever the future may have in store, the American volunteer will not be found wanting. Never again, upon the battle-fields of their own land, will Americans be pitted against Americans; but the question now is, as a recent writer puts it, "whether American volunteers of the future shall enter upon the campaign against a foreign foe, when war is forced upon them, as an army of well-trained citizen soldiery, or, speaking from a military point of view, as a heterogeneous mob. Conditions have changed since military men now living acquired their experience, and they will continue to change. Unless our methods of preparation are in keeping with the times, we must one day pay dearly for the oversight."

This very nearly came true in the war of '98. "Preparedness" would have saved the fighters of Santiago from the dismal aftermath of sickness and distress. Safety must be gained by foresight.

It is due to the past valor and the present efficiency of the American volunteer that this foresight shall never again be lacking. What is worth having is worth defending, and the price of liberty, as we know from national experience, is eternal vigilance.

"The past at least is secure!" Whatever the future of the American soldier shall be, its successes, its changes, or its failures cannot rob him of the luster of his ancient glory or becloud the record of his old renown. The progress of invention in the science and art of war may render unnecessary the "serried lines" that have for many a century made up the poetry and panoply of battle; smokeless powder and noiseless guns may add to the terrors of the fight the horror of a death-dealing silence; military maneuvers may become but the accompaniments to the horrid hiss of steam and the silent mystery of electricity; enthusiasm may be but the working-out of a scientific formula, and valor but a thing of cogs and cranks; but spite of all mechanical advances, and of every progressing change, the American soldier will be the soldier still. Still will he be patient, courageous, impetuous; as stout of heart, as stern of will, as full of pluck and heroism, as when in the days gone by he stood for liberty at Lexington and Bunker Hill, at Monmouth and Saratoga and Yorktown; for stubborn spirit and unconquerable arm at Lundy's Lane and New Orleans; for dash and daring at Monterey and Buena Vista and Chapultepec; for patriotism, valor, undying loyalty and deathless fame at Shiloh and Gettysburg, at Antietam and Chickamauga, at Malvern Hill and Petersburg and Atlanta; for desperate bravery, unconquerable even in savage death, at the Withlacoochee and the Little Big Horn; for humanity, justice, and the liberation of a people at El Caney and Manila and the heights of San Juan; and, above all, for generosity, for manliness, and the charity that never faileth — the nineteenth century chivalry that held out to a suffering neighbor the strong and generous hand of '98, even as it had extended to a conquered foe the hands of brotherly love and forgiveness across the furled flags and the silent drums of historic Appomattox.

www.ingramcontent.com/pod-product-compliance
Lightning Source LLC
Chambersburg PA
CBHW021953220426
43663CB00007B/800